CISTERCIAN FATHERS SERIES: NUMBER FORTY-NINE

Gertrud the Great of Helfta
Spiritual Exercises

CISTERCIAN FATHERS SERIES: NUMBER FORTY-NINE

GERTRUD THE GREAT OF HELFTA

SPIRITUAL EXERCISES

Translation, Introduction, Notes and Indexes

by

Gertrud Jaron Lewis and Jack Lewis

Cistercian Publications
Kalamazoo
1989

A translation based on *Gertrude d'Helfta, Oeuvres Spirituelles*,
tome 1: *Les Exercices*. Texte latin. Introduction et notes
par Jacques Hourlier et Albert Schmitt. Sources Chrétiennes 127
(Paris: Editions du Cerf, 1967).

Gertrud of Helfta (1256–1301/02)

Available in Britain and Europe from
A.R. Mowbray & Co Ltd
St Thomas House Becket Street
Oxford OX 1 1SJ

Available elsewhere (including Canada) from
Cistercian Publications
WMU Station
Kalamazoo, Michigan 49008

The work of Cistercian Publications is made possible in part
by support from Western Michigan University
to the Institute of Cistercian Studies.

Library of Congress Cataloging in Publication Data

Gertrude, the Great, Saint, 1256–1302.
[Exercitia spiritualia. Tome 1. English]
Spiritual exercises / Gertrude the Great of Helfta; translation,
introduction, notes, and indexes by Gertrud Jaron Lewis and Jack Lewis.
p. 147 cm. — (Cistercian Fathers series; no. 49)
Translation of: tome 1 of Exercitia spiritualia.
Includes index.
ISBN 0-87907-049-8.   ISBN 0-87907-449-3 (pbk.)
1. Spiritual life—Middle Ages, 600–1500.   I. Lewis, Gertrud
Jaron, 1931–.   II. Lewis, Jack, 1929–   .   III. Title.   IV. Series.
BX2349.G42513 1988   248.3—dc19   88-18949

*Typeset by the Carmelites of Indianapolis
Printed in the United States of America*

TABLE OF CONTENTS

ACKNOWLEDGEMENTS

This translation of Gertrud of Helfta's *Exercitia spiritualia* is based on the most recent critical edition of the Latin text: *Gertrud d'Helfta, Oeuvres Spirituelles*, vol. I: *Les Exercices*, ed. by Jacques Hourlier and Albert Schmitt. Sources Chrétiennes 127, Paris 1967, which includes an excellent introduction into authorship, reception, language, and themes. Line numbering in our translation approximates that of this Sources Chrétiennes text as closely we as could manage.

Additionally, we regularly took advantage of the good grasp of the basic meaning of Gertrud's text by M. Columba Hart, osb (*Spiritual Exercises*, Westminster 1956) and found Hart's introduction, commentary and notes very helpful.

We thank Sr. Miriam Schmitt, osb, for her deep insights into the text, especially those concerning monastic life, many of which we have integrated into our introduction.

The thorough editing as well as many helpful suggestions by E. Rozanne Elder are most gratefully acknowledged.

G.J.L. and J.L.

TABLE OF ABBREVIATIONS

Bernard, SC	Bernard of Clairvaux, *On the Song of Songs* I–IV (CF 4, 7, 31, 41). Kalamazoo, Mich. 1971–1980).
DSp	*Dictionnaire de spiritualité ascétique et mystique, doctrine et histoire.* Ed. Marcel Viller et al. Paris 1937 ff.
ExspSCh	Gertrude d'Helfta, *Les Exercices* (Latin-Français). Eds. Jacques Hourlier, Albert Schmitt (Sources Chrétiennes 127). Paris 1967.
Hart	*The Exercises of Saint Gertrude.* Introd., commentary and trans. Columba Hart, OSB Westminster, Maryland 1956.
JB	*The Jerusalem Bible.* Ed. Alexander Jones et. al. Garden City, N.Y. (1966).
Legatus	Gertrud of Helfta, *Legatus divinae pietatis*, quoted after its latest critical edition in Sources Chrétiennes:
	Gertrude d'Helfta, *Oeuvres spirituelles* (Latin-Français). Le Héraut I et II (139), III (143). Ed. Pierre Doyère. Paris 1968. Le Héraut IV (255) and V (331). Eds. Jean-Marie Clément, Bénédicte Masquelier, Bernard de Vregille. Paris 1978 and 1986.
Liturgie-Lexikon	Gerhard Podhradsky, *Lexikon der Liturgie.* Innsbruck / Vienna / Munich (1962).
LThK	*Lexikon für Theologie und Kirche.* Ed. Michael Buchberger et al. (First ed. 1930–1938). Second rev. ed. Josef Höfer, Karl Rahner et al. Freiburg i.B. 1957 –1968. Repr. 1986.

Lüers   Grete Lüers, *Die Sprache der deutschen Mystik des Mittelalters im Werke der Mechthild von Magdeburg.* München 1926. Repr. Darmstadt 1966.

Metz   René Metz, *La Consécration des vierges dans l'Église romaine* (Bibl. de l'Inst. de Droit canonique de Strasbourg 4). Strasbourg 1954.

Pontificale   *Pontificale Romanum.* Mechlin 1873.

RB   *The Rule of St. Benedict in Latin and English.* With notes and thematic index. Ed. Timothy Fry OSB. Collegeville, Minn. (1981).

Vocabulaire monastique Jean Leclercq, *Études sur le vocabulaire monastique du moyen-âge* (Studia Anselmiana 48). Rome 1961.

INTRODUCTION

Gertrud of Helfta's *Spiritual Exercises* consists of meditations, rituals, prayers, instructions on how to pray, chants, hymns, and litanies—in short, ruminations of a medieval mystic on various themes based on Scripture and liturgy. The Carthusian Lanspergius (Johannes Gerecht from Landsberg, Bavaria) first published Gertrud's *Exercitia spiritualia* under this name as part of her entire work in Cologne in 1536.

While the title may not be Gertrud's own, it seems appropriate in view of her biographer's statement in Book One of Gertrud of Helfta's *Legatus divinae pietatis* that Gertrud composed various pieces of writing for the benefit of the Helfta community, among others *documenta spiritualium exercitationum*, 'examples of spiritual exercises' (*Legatus* I. 1, 2, 36). The term 'spiritual exercises' in contrast to 'bodily exercises' is defined in a passage in William of Saint Thierry's *Golden Epistle*[1] that Gertrud apparently knew under the authorship of St Bernard of Clairvaux. William recommends both these exercises to the novices he writes for: 'It is not spiritual exercises that exist for the sake of bodily exercises but bodily for the spiritual . . . (XXII.85); and 'Allot to each other and every hour in accordance with the rule of the common observance its own exercises, spiritual when they are due and bodily when they are due' (XXIX. 109).

The division of the text of the *Spiritual Exercises* honors the sacred number seven, which signifies fullness and perfection. The chapters are quite

---

1. Trans. Theodore Berkeley. Introd. J.M. Déchanet, CF 12 (Kalamazoo 1980).

unequal in length, and frequently the same material is dealt with in more than one chapter. The Latin chapter headings are not original and must be considered generally inadequate.[2] Our own titles are intended to serve only as rough guides for each exercise. A discussion of the main points of each chapter is provided at the conclusion of this introduction.

THE AUTHOR

The author of the *Spiritual Exercises*, Gertrud the Great of Helfta (1256–1301/02), should no longer need a lengthy introduction.[3] She is one of the so-called Helfta mystics, the other two being her older contemporaries, Mechthild of Magdeburg and Mechthild of Hackeborn. Under the superb guidance of their abbess Gertrud of Hackeborn, who was not herself a writer, this Benedictine monastery became a center of mysticism and culture in thirteenth century Germany.

Gertrud of Helfta's writing includes the *Legatus divinae pietatis*, 'The Messenger of Divine Loving-Kindness', a large work in five parts of which only Book Two was written by Gertrud's own hand. Book One represents Gertrud's *vita*. Books Three to Five reflect her thoughts but were in part composed from notes taken by her sisters following Gertrud's dictation or ruminations. The only other extant work of Gertrud is the *Spiritual Exercises*, whose manuscript has been lost but whose authenticity was satisfactorily established by comparison with Book Two of the *Legatus*, which does have manuscript authority.

---

2. Cf. ExspSCh, 44.

3. Gertrud of Helfta and her contemporaries have been brought to attention in the writings of Sister M. Jeremy Finnegan (esp. *Scholars and Mystics*, Chicago 1962) and of Caroline Walker Bynum (esp. *Jesus as Mother. Studies in the Spirituality of the High Middle Ages*. Berkeley/Los Angeles/London 1982. Pb. 1984). Despite recent scholarship (notably, the introductions and appendices of the SCh-edition of the complete works of Gertrud the Great) and after over one hundred years of the appearance of the first critical edition of the Helfta mystics by the Benedictines of Solesmes, Gertrud of Helfta is still sometimes wrongly identified because of lingering confusion between Gertrud the Great and her abbess, Gertrud of Hackeborn.

THE LANGUAGE

The *Exercitia spiritualia* was composed in medieval Latin prose. Lanspergius' first edition of the work in 1536 included his own translation of three Middle High German passages into Latin. These short passages, some three hundred words altogether, are all that remains of Gertrud's vernacular writing. They strike the reader as somewhat less formal than the surrounding Latin text and are included in our translation as an alternative reading.

A skilled writer, Gertrud masters the Latin of her time and composes her work with extreme care and with an eye on detail. A real feeling for language is apparent. At times, Gertrud seems to express herself almost naturally in rhythmic prose, and her text, especially the seventh Exercise, also includes passages in verse. As Alois Maria Haas and Kurt Ruh have shown, mystical language, especially that of women writers, often spontaneously erupts in verse and rhythm to express mystical spirituality.[4]

One notable feature of Gertrud's rich vocabulary is variety in naming God (or Christ). Examples include: O serenest light, utmost bright morning (V,32) . . . O my most dulcet morning (IV, 295) . . . fountain of wisdom, fountain of light (III, 96 and 114) . . . flowering spring day filled with life (III, 63f.) . . . oak of hope (I, 199) . . . consuming fire (IV, 68 from Dt 4:24 and Hebr 12:29) . . . splendor of the divine sun (III,8) and fulgent spring day that knows no waning (ibid.). In passing we notice that Gertrud gives a partial solution to the problem of a patriarchal God image and thereby offers us a lead for using such creative appellations for the Divine.

As these examples suggest, Gertrud's images can at times be daring. She speaks of the earthquake of her heart (I, 9f.); of the 'voracious flame' of God's living love into which she wants to be thrown (IV, 406); and of the fiery charity of the Holy Spirit (III, 324). Among her favorite expressions are those with *medulla*, such as 'the marrow of compassion' (VII, 403), with fat or fatness following the Old Testament usage, such as 'your face fattens the souls of the saints' (VI, 227f.), and with viscera,[5] such as 'the holy four

---

4. Haas, *Sermo mysticus. Studien zur Theologie und Sprache der Deutschen Mystik* (Fribourg, Switzerland 1979) 67–103 [passim]; and Ruh, *Vorbemerkungen zu einer neuen Geschichte der abendländischen Mystik im Mittelalter* (Munich 1982) 3–32 [passim].

5. While we seriously considered alternative translations of *viscera* (including 'bowels' and 'interior being') we settled for 'viscera' as best suited to Gertrud's imagery.

winged animals all of whose viscera belch forth [God's] praise' (VI, 462ff.).
Gertrud's prose is sometimes criticized for its abundance of sweet-sounding
adjectives, and yet the reader of the *Exercitia* will find passages such as this:
'you have raptured my spirit so that my body is now rotting and stinks like
a dungpit' (VI, 612f.). Among the images used as motifs throughout the
Exercitia, those using dawn (*aurora*), dew (*rora*), and the greening of spring
(*vernans* etc.), while commonplace in medieval mystical works, are particu-
larly beautiful.

The question inevitably arises as to how this cloistered nun, who entered
the monastery as a child of five and presumably never left it even once
because of the strict rule of *stabilitas loci*, could with such rich skill master
poetic prose. The answer is to be found precisely in her monastic upbringing
and in the daily liturgy celebrated by the sisters. The highly cultured Helfta
abbey provided Gertrud with classical schooling in the seven liberal arts and
led her to study theology as well as to do exegetical work of her own on the
Scripture. The community's daily chanting of the psalms and extensive
reading of Bible passages in the Divine Office, and the daily *lectio* on Scripture imbued her, furthermore, during all her life, with the language and imagery of the Old and New Testament. Therefore, most of her metaphorical
language can be traced back to Scripture passages, as the numerous notes in
the text indicate. Indeed, some passages in the *Spiritual Exercises* (notably in
the *Jubilus*-Chapter) are remarkable for the fact that biblical allusions are
rare or absent.

The great variety of scriptural passages cited in this text shows how
thoroughly familiar Gertrud is with the Bible. But her close association with
the Scripture goes far beyond her switching from a Psalm text to Luke,
from Jeremiah to Revelations or St Paul. Gertrud of Helfta appears to have
lived life fully though vicariously by living with and through the Scripture.
To take one example from among many, she often makes a biblical word
her own: Gertrud uses the phrase of the crafty steward of the parable (Lk
16:3) out of context and applies it to her own condition of having nowhere
to turn but to Christ: 'Dig? I am not strong enough. Go begging? I should be
too ashamed' (VII, 460f.). In addition to quoting passages from the Old and
New Testament, Gertrud also relies on the Bible as the basis for her imagi-
native grasp of reality. While she may have been familiar with dew, raindrops, and the hedge (mentioned in *Legatus* Book Two), we cannot auto-
matically assume that Gertrud ever experienced overflowing rivers or whirl-

winds. Rather, it is the biblical imagery that she integrates as part of her own experience.

While Gertrud makes the biblical word an essential part of her meditation, her poetic yet often stark language and imagery still carries her own imprint. Although strongly influenced by liturgy and Scripture, as are most medieval christian spiritual works, Gertrud's exquisite style and accomplished use of rhetoric cannot be mistaken for that of anyone else.

Our notes include both the Bible references from the ExspSCh-edition and those given in Hart's translation. We have also added some of our own. In doing so we used the Vulgate to decide on which biblical passage St Gertrud relies. But we assume that many more allusions to Scripture could be documented. The frequent Psalm passages are quoted according to the Latin Vulgate with the JB numbers in parentheses. The appended index provides a survey of Gertrud's Bible references.

FEMININE SPIRITUALITY

Perhaps even more than the *Legatus*, St Gertrud's *Spiritual Exercises* reveals to the reader a woman in monastic life who is completely conscious of and committed to her own womanhood. Her attitude has to be understood as extraordinary because the psalms and, in fact, all the liturgical prayers, address God from the viewpoint of a male worshipper or a male sinner. And there were actually medieval women writers, including Gertrud's friend in Helfta, Mechthild of Hackeborn (cf., for instance, *Liber specialis gratiae* I. 19), who consciously wished to alter their natural gender so that they could adapt to the patriarchal structure of the church and truly be 'sons of God.'[6] But Gertrud, while she lived in a church that had during most of its history demanded that its faithful take on the *persona* of a male, insists on fully living her femininity. Her female self-confidence is such that she sees no reason to make an apology or give an explanation, as if speaking to God from a woman's point of view were the most natural thing to do.

All seven chapters of her *Exercitia spiritualia*, whether Gertrud speaks directly to God in prayer or addresses her readers and community members

---

6. Cf. also Bynum, *Jesus*, 138f.

in instruction, are written from the feminine perspective. Usually this comes out explicitly in the grammatical endings, as when she prays, for instance, 'that in the violence of living love I may become your prisoner (*captiva*, a female prisoner) for all time' (VII, 65f.). At other places the appropriate feminine noun is inserted, for instance, when Gertrud sees herself as the 'prodigal daughter' (IV, 184), or as the 'adopted daughter' (V, 510). In her *Legatus* (V. 32, 2, 3), we even find Gertrud adapting what had become a topos in the spiritual prose of her time: the well-known image of John leaning against the breast of Christ at the Last Supper is altered to represent herself as a young girl (*puella*) taking John's place.[7] Such phrases lose much in an English translation unless a special effort is made to distinguish between male and female. Our translation makes the distinction wherever possible.

Gertrud's self-confident female attitude is perhaps more remarkable in that nuns in the choir used masculine nouns and pronouns to refer to themselves. Each office ends: *Divinum auxilium maneat semper nobiscum. Et cum fratribus nostris absentibus* (May God's help abide with us always. And with our absent brothers). Gertrud thus includes adjustments which the liturgy did not provide for.[8] There are two places where Gertrud, in fact, relapses into this generally adopted male *persona*. In Chapter Seven she abruptly and perhaps inadvertently shifts to the masculine gender in speaking about herself (cf. 155 and 158); and one time (VII, 684) she prays that 'brotherly charity' may be increased in her. These two passages let us appreciate all the more Gertrud's conscious effort throughout to maintain the feminine perspective.

The reader cannot help wondering whether St Gertrud's unabashed femininity in religious matters has been a cause of the highly jagged reception her work has experienced during the last seven hundred years.[9] And perhaps it is equally her strong female stance that has given rise to accusations of 'naïveté' (Ernest Hello)[10] and 'puérilités' (Pierre Doyère).[11]

---

7. This Christ-John image also became the theme of numerous sculptural representations that played a great role in the convents of the fourteenth century.

8. We are indebted to E. Rozanne Elder for this contribution.

9. Cf. 'Succès posthume' in ExspSCh, 14–38. Cf. also G.J.L., 'Zur Rezeption des Werkes Gertruds von Helfta' in *Kontroversen, alte und neue*, ed. Albrecht Schöne (Tübingen 1986) vol. 6:3–10.

10. Hello, *Physionomie des saints* (1st ed. 1875) (Paris 1920) 369.

11. DSp vol. 6:col. 334.

As is common in medieval works, both by men and women writers, we readily find images in the *Spiritual Exercises* relating to the feminine aspects of God, such as the biblical metaphors with God as a mother. But also here Gertrud goes one step further than did most writers. In much of her seventh Exercise, for instance, she addresses God as feminine. Gertrud speaks to God or Christ through personifications: Goodness (*bonitas*), Charity (*caritas*), Cherishing-love (*dilectio*), Compassion (*misericordia*), Peace (*pax*), Loving-kindness (*pietas*), Wisdom (*sapientia*), and Truth (*veritas*). The fact that each term is a feminine noun in Latin permits Gertrud to use feminine pronouns and endings in the context. While it would be anachronistic to suggest that Gertrud challenges the Father-God image, her choice of mostly feminine attributes of God, given her own female self-confidence, should not be interpreted as accidental. St Gertrud, like other spiritual writers, uses only analogies, of course, to approach divine mystery; but patriarchal God-images are themselves analogies. By employing simultaneously both male and female attributes for God, Gertrud illustrates a very healthy approach to a concept of God that goes beyond the gender issue.

MAJOR THEMES

Gertrud of Helfta is not a systematic writer, and most of the themes we encounter in her *Spiritual Exercises* are typical for a medieval work of mysticism. Nevertheless, Gertrud adds emphases and perspectives of note.

St Gertrud's mysticism is typically Christ-centered. Christ in his human-ity forms the basis and focus of all of Gertrud's writing. The human nature of Christ as one with the Spirit and as part of the Trinity, while still 'in the substance of my flesh' (VI, 107, 180, 418), represents the pivotal point of Gertrud's mystical life.[12] And she bases her bridal imagery on Christ's human nature being retained in his heavenly state.[13]

Bridal imagery (*Brautmystik*) is derived from the Song of Songs and has, in fact, had a long tradition in the history of the church. Mystical language, of course, has to be symbolical since the mystical experience is *per se* ineffable;

---

12. Cf. André Rayez, 'La Mystique féminine et l'humanité du Christ'. DSp 7/1: cols 1088 f.
13. Cf. ExspSCh, 208 f., n. 7.

and the symbol of spousal love at least comes close to describing the mystical relationship between God and the soul. During the late middle ages, the strongest proponent of this language of love is St Bernard of Clairvaux, an obvious influence on St Gertrud.[14] Gertrud of Helfta's own use of the symbol of nuptial union, the marital embrace, is neither shy nor prudish. Her vocabulary frequently has sexual overtones, yet her powerful style does not permit cheap sentimentality. She refers to herself as *sponsa et uxor*, i.e. not only bride but explicitly wife. A mature conjugal love that has abandoned the frivolous aspects of bridal courtship is at the centre of Gertrud's imagery. And in this context of the *unio mystica*, we find some of her most beautiful and joyous images.

While Gertrud thus focuses on Christ's glorified human nature, she does not emphasize the belief that human nature in general is restored through the incarnation of Christ. She often distinguished between the 'rotten body' and the spirit (cf., for instance, VI, 612f.). The body-soul dichotomy remains unreconciled in the *Spiritual Exercises*.

As is the case in most spiritual works of this period, Gertrud's text unequivocally defines the *summum bonum* in terms of the biblical 'seeing God face to face'. Thus, sight, vision, face, and countenance constitute an essential part of this work's vocabulary. The desire to reach God *sine impedimento* (without any hindrance) is reiterated throughout as direct contact with the Divine remains her goal.

Closely connected to the theme of vision is that of light. Drawn from Bible images, especially from St John's mystical language, light in its various forms and expressions is of central importance in medieval mysticism in general. Many striking images in the *Exercitia* center on God as radiant light, as the true light, the fountain of everlasting light, the source of light itself. Christ who is our enlightenment dazzles us through the brightness of his light. He is himself the beautiful dawn of divinity, the sun of justice.

---

14. It remains to be determined what influence the wide-spread German prose translation of the Canticum by the abbot Williram (†1085) of Ebersberg, Bavaria, and the subsequent commentary by the German abesses Rilindis and Herrat of Landsperg had on the Helfta community. Their commentary was aimed directly at nuns who were told to see themselves as brides of Christ. (Cf. *Das Hohe Lied übersetzt von Willeram, erklärt von Rilindis und Herrat, Äbtissinnen* (1147–1196), ed. Josef Haupt (Vienna 1864), VIII.) Based on Williram's translation, there is as well a twelfth century anonymous German poetic version of the Song of Songs, the *St. Trudperter Hohe Lied*, whose main feature is a pervasive bridal imagery.

For St Gertrud, life—always seen as positive—provides a dominant key
term in her work. In typically medieval christian fashion, Gertrud defines
human life backwards, so to speak. The motifs *usque ad finem* and *in hora
mortis* emphasize this life's certain end. Life gains meaning through its consummation in death, while baptism, confirmation and communion are
sources of spiritual rebirth and renewal in this life. Life on earth is
represented in the traditional image of a pilgrimage whose destination is our
ultimate home. As this image suggests, life is anything but static. Gertrud
stresses the necessity of constant spiritual growth; she loathes nothing more
than barrenness or stagnation, and she prays: 'Lord, free me from all sterility
of mind' (IV, 175ff.). The tension between *now* and *then* or *here* and *there*
runs through all the text. Faith functions as a staff on the journey's way, and
the frequent term faith is more often than not combined with *rectus* or *in-
teger*, i.e. a faith that for her is, without any doubt, the right one and has integrity (wholeness).

It is this upright loving faith that causes human beings to adhere to God
with an unbreakable bond. Gertrud expresses this inseparable adherence
persistently with the vocabulary of being glued, even of sticking like cement,
to God. While somewhat unusual for today's reader, this image of the
'ghostly glue', as Evelyn Underhill states, is a frequent alternative to the
bridal imagery in the mystic's endeavor to speak of 'the bond between the
soul and the Absolute'.[15]

St Gertrud understands asceticism (*abnegare, abstrahere, abstinentia, adnibilare*) not as self-chastisement but as self-denial with its important implica-
tion of making amends (*suppletio, supplere*). Ascetic life in the Helfta community did not go to the extremes reported by or of later ascetic-minded
mystics. Rather, as Gertrud states, asceticism implies working hard and incessantly at freeing oneself from all the fetters and shackles that fasten
everyone to ungodly things.

This process of inner liberation implies mortification, dying to oneself in
order to live for God alone (III, 149). That is, paradoxically, through ascetic
death life is gained: 'Already I have perished from myself into you, and,
living, I have died' (VI, 700). Many passages throughout Gertrud's writings
allude to the complex notion of *mors mystica* (what the german mystics call

---

15. Evelyn Underhill, *Mysticism*, 1st ed. 1910 (New York 1953), 427.

Minnetod). The mystic's ascetic striving becomes meaningful only if dying constitutes a beginning rather than an end, a paradoxical reversal of death and life which, in the final analysis, goes back to the mystery of the cross.[16]

It is from this perspective of dying to oneself that Gertrud of Helfta understands 'inner freedom'. *Libertas cordis* is Gertrud's unique characteristic and her most important theme in general.[17] While the concept of freedom is mainly discussed in the *Legatus*, in the *Spiritual Exercises*, too, it plays an important role. Gertrud, in a prayer for forgiveness asks that there be restored in her that 'freedom of spirit' by which she has been 'set free' (VII, 495ff.). And she is always concerned that her heart remain 'detached and free' (VII, 398).

Encountering the Divine leads Gertrud to what may well be the most beautiful mystical *jubilus* to be found in all of medieval mystical literature. The *jubilus* (the term is presumably derived from the extended melodic form of the chanted Alleluia) represents an outburst of ecstatic joy and praise of God, which follows the deepest mystical experience. Gertrud's *jubilus* is of an incomparable poetic beauty with an almost contagious effect on the reader. At its best—and this is the case in St Gertrud's extended jubilation—the *jubilus* has a cosmic dimension, uniting the entire universe in the joy of the Lord. We witness in this *jubilus* an explosion of joy of which only a mystic is capable who simultaneously can state: 'I have considered all worldly joy like mud on my feet' (V, 99f.).

THE SEVEN EXERCISES

The importance of Gertrud of Helfta's *Spiritual Exercises* goes far beyond the limited audience of contemporary nuns for whom the work was, presumably, intended. Gertrud's short volume of prayers and meditations and instructions on a life of prayer is a true jewel among medieval spiritual prose

---

16. Cf. Alois Maria Haas, 'Mors mystica' *Freiburger Zeitschrift für Philosophie und Theologie* 23 (1976) 304–392 [passim].

17. Cf. also Pierre Doyère, DSp 6 (1967) cols 331–339.

pieces. And to read this book only to analyze its role in the history of christian spirituality would be to miss the point.

The first four of the seven Exercises are based freely on liturgical rites. Specifically, Chapter One recalls some aspects of the sacrament of baptism, while, roughly, Chapters Two to Four relate to the rituals of clothing, consecration, and profession that a cloistered medieval nun (and likely anyone in a religious community) would have experienced as milestones in the monastic life. Liturgical celebrations of such high impact for the individual remain ingrained in the mind. By recalling individual steps in these liturgies, then, Gertrud is sure to stimulate an immediate positive response from her sisters in community who will easily remember the spiritual and emotional significance of these rites in their own lives. Chapters Five to Seven take the Divine Office as their liturgical background.

But the *Spiritual Exercises* can be used by anyone, not only by women and men in monastic life familiar with the rituals mentioned. Their foremost basis is a spiritual one, hence they may serve as a general aid in meditation and prayer. The following notes are intended to help the reader understand the monastic terminology; they also point to the special themes of each individual exercise. (Footnotes throughout the text provide further guidance.)

THE FIRST EXERCISE: REBIRTH

Meditating on the theme of rebirth, Gertrud of Helfta calls to mind the ceremony of baptism (and of confirmation in as much as the latter constitutes a renewal of the baptismal vows). The author encourages her readers to envisage an actual baptismal ceremony by directing us with her rubrics through various stages of the liturgy. Simultaneously, however, by not quite following the sequence of the actual steps of a baptism and by omitting a number of steps, she implicitly stresses that it is, after all, an inner renewal, a meditation, that this Exercise is concerned with.

The stages of the ceremony that the author invites the reader to memorize or meditate upon in this chapter are the following:

reading the Creed (13ff.);

saying the formula of the exorcism (35ff.);

signing oneself with the sign of the cross (52ff.);
laying on of hands (however not by the priest but rather by Jesus) (61ff.);
tasting the salt of wisdom (87ff.);
receiving [Mary as] a godmother (114ff.);
getting a name (135ff.);
being immersed in the baptismal fountain (141ff.);
anointing with chrism (151ff.);
clothing with the white baptismal gown (165ff.);
receiving the lighted candle (171ff.).

In between, Gertrud inserts directions for welcoming the guardian angel (70ff.) and taking up the standard of the crucifix (105ff.), which do not constitute a part of the actual baptismal ceremony.

What is essential to St Gertrud in the stages enumerated above is the new beginning in the Spirit. The text abounds in words like renew, recreate, reshape, remake, regenerate, restore, that denote the mystical rebirth in God. Simultaneously she gives a glimpse of what this new life entails: integrity of faith, triumph over the enemy, unyielding perseverance, and freedom of spirit. Gertrud thus simultaneously introduces the major themes that she develops in the following Exercises, such as the bridal theme, the longing of being at leisure with God, and the desire of seeing God face to face for eternity.

The last third of the First Exercise (178ff.) suggests beautiful meditations for use after receiving communion. Gertrud concentrates on the life-giving power of this sacrament, thus integrating the Eucharist as essential into the theme of rebirth.

THE SECOND EXERCISE: SPIRITUAL CONVERSION

The theme of spiritual conversion in the second rather short chapter takes the anniversary of the 'clothing' of the nun in monastic habit as a basis for meditation. Various instructions for prayer and meditation are again given in the form of precise rubrics, such as 'At this point, fall down at the feet of Jesus' (50) or 'At this point, hide in Christ Jesus' (41). Although similar in formulation to the liturgical directives, these rubrics are clearly of a spiritual nature.

While the symbol of receiving the habit implies for the author the accept-ance of various other aspects of the monastic life, it is easy to transpose her prayers and thoughts out of the immediate monastic context and to under-stand them as general christian guidelines for spiritual conversion. In Gertrud's context, conversion means renouncing the world in such a way that nothing that is not Christ remains of any concern. Through the school of love, she sees a steady growth of love, religion, simplicity, and holiness as the explicit goal.

Gertrud ends the Exercise with a prayer that contains the image of 'us, your women servants' running 'manfully' on the path of God's kingdom.

THE THIRD EXERCISE: DEDICATION OF THE SELF

This chapter celebrates the anniversary of the monastic consecration. The 'Rite of the consecration of virgins', going back to the fourth century, con-sisted of an 'elaborate ritual',[18] which took place during mass and was nor-mally conducted by a bishop.[19] It consisted of three essential parts: the solemn entrance procession; the blessing of the veil, crown, and rings; and the solemn, time-honored prayers which were followed by the issuing of the insignia.

The stages of this liturgy freely referred to by Gertrud in this chapter are the following:

the invitatory 'Come' (106ff.);
the litany (113ff.);
the triple *Suscipe me* (receive me) (192ff.);
the consecration preface (200ff.);
the investiture with veil (259), crown (271), and ring (288)—which are considered the essential symbols of the consecration;
the episcopal blessing (317ff.);
the bishop commending the nun to the care of the abbess (338ff.);
the hymn *Te Deum laudamus* (354ff.).

---

18. Hart, 27.
19. For the liturgy of the Consecration see *Pontificale*, 126-149, Hart, 27-32, and Metz *passim*.

14   *Spiritual Exercises of Gertrud the Great of Helfta*

Each of these points is slightly altered and adapted by Gertrud to lead the reader to meditation. The author, for instance, has the Lord in place of the bishop commend her to Mary, instead of to the abbess. And while St Gertrud repeats much of the ritual of the Consecration, she significantly omits the lengthy *anathema* traditionally pronounced by the bishop at the end of the ceremony.[20]

The chapter's theme is the spiritual matrimony. There is a joyous tone of spring-like merriment throughout as the prose text resembles a song of love. Christ, the bridegroom, is the exemplar of radiance, the sun. Notably, since Christ's desire is as great as the bride's, this marriage of love consists of a mutual exchange of vows. The coupling of the chaste love, this kiss of love, seals an inseparable union. The bond of love between the two spouses is compared to the glue that unites the Father to the Son. And the true spouse and wife, made fertile, brings forth the fruits of life. The wedding imagery ends with the metaphor of the exulted mystical dance in heaven.

THE FOURTH EXERCISE: FOLLOWING CHRIST

A nun's profession is the liturgical basis for this fourth chapter, which means that the normal order of monastic events is reversed since in real monastic life profession precedes consecration.[21] Until the Council of Trent (1545–1563), a novice was permitted to take the vows of profession only at or after the age of twelve, while consecration had the age requirement of twenty-five years. The profession of vows may be understood as the human response to a divine call, and the consecration is seen as the divine blessing for a person's vow. St Gertrud, in abandoning the strict chronology of monastic events by having the memory of 'profession' follow that of 'consecration', may have followed a progressive order of spiritual significance to her.[22]

---

20. *Pontificale*, 147.
21. Cf. Hart, 55.
22. We are indebted to S. Miriam Schmitt for clarification of this passage.

The author's rubrics concern the following stages in the ceremony of the monastic profession;

the invitatory (44ff.);

the litany (100ff.), again in Gertrud's own version and different from the one in Chapter Three;

the act of profession (233ff.);

the acceptance of the monastic rule (258ff.);

the threefold *Suscipe* (259, 263, 267);

the clothing with the monastic habit (287ff.).

This exercise ends with meditations for use after communion (312ff.) and thanksgiving with the *Magnificat* (372ff.), the hymn attributed to Mary in Lk 1:46ff.

The dominant theme is that of becoming a true follower of Christ with him as a brother, guide, and companion on the road, and assisted by the many saints Gertrud calls upon in her litany. In her passionate desire to turn her frail human condition to God alone, the mystic repeatedly prays, as follows: teach me how to fear you, show me how to love you, instruct me how to follow you. God, the all-consuming fire, will turn darkness into light. The 'prodigal daughter' yearns to be fashioned after God's own heart and to be granted an unconquered spirit and a steadfast soul in running the racetrack that promises God as the prize.

THE FIFTH EXERCISE: MYSTICAL UNION

In this chapter we encounter the full array of mystical vocabulary that attempts to describe the ineffable mystical experience of union with God, the fruition achieved through the coupling of the Word with the soul. Gertrud's central metaphor stands within the tradition of *Brautmystik*. Having concluded the nuptial contract with the Lord, the mystic is burning for the kiss of her immortal spouse, for the wedding embrace in the innermost bedchamber of the heart. With the Lord as husband, the offspring of this marital union will be perfect love; it will mean becoming one spirit with God. Images like a spark in fire and a drop of water in the ocean describe beautifully the total absorption in God. Gertrud uses the analogy of the spiritual senses to express this one-ness, so that tasting, touching, and seeing the divine lead to ecstasy. Being stilled by the presence of God, who is the 'true today', the soul will be fully at leisure with love.

Inserted in this prayerful and ecstatic text on the *unio mystica* is a discourse (292–463) that makes use of the seven canonical hours. The underlying image here is that of a school of love that progressively leads to mystical fruition.

At Lauds, pray that you be taught the art of love (292ff.);

at Prime, that you be led into the school of love with God as teacher and master (311ff.);

at Terce, that you learn the alphabet with which the Spirit writes his law of love on your heart (330ff.);

at Sext, that you learn to know the Lord not only by syllables but also by theory (356ff.);

at None, that you be accepted into the militia of love and bound by oath (377ff.);

at Vespers, that you march in the armor of love and triumph over evil (401ff.); and

at Compline, that you become oblivious to the world and be consummated in loving union with God (434ff.).

The liturgy of the Divine Office that played an essential part in Gertrud of Helfta's own spiritual growth is thus seen as a means to attain to the mystical union.

This Exercise, located pretty much at the center of the book, represents the very essence of the mystic's striving.

THE SIXTH EXERCISE: jubilus

Although not free of all influences, this Exercise is the most independent of the seven chapters. It is neither based on any liturgical rite nor does it rely heavily on the Scripture, as does the remainder of the work. It is especially noteworthy for combining bridal imagery with a musical theme. Singing and instrumental music (cithara, cymbal, lyre, psaltery, and organ) play an important role in the text.

Formally, this chapter is marked by parallel passages: a section dominated by the formula 'Bless the Lord' (98ff.); a section in the form of a hymn (135ff); then a section dominated by the formula 'Praise the Lord' (229ff.); and a second 'Bless the Lord' passage (380ff.). After these comes the grandiose *jubilus* section, which stretches from lines 421 to 489.

The *jubilus* consists of praise, jubilation, and thanksgiving for all the good God has done. Written in an exulted language, the *jubilus* anticipates the eternal radiant praise before the face of the Lord. The mystic here calls on heaven and earth to join her in this joyous celebration: shake off the dust, lift yourselves up, sing glory before God's countenance, she exhorts us. Calling herself an atom of God's universe, St Gertrud wishes that all creation were within her power so that she could unite all things in the glory of God's praise.

THE SEVENTH EXERCISE: LIFE IN DEATH

The final Exercise is dominated by the theme of death, treated, in a way that is true to the Christian paradox, as life-giving.

Liturgically, this chapter (like the fifth Exercise) relies on the Divine Office, and it structures its thoughts according to the daily monastic prayers. Gertrud of Helfta here matches meditations at the seven canonical hours with stations of Christ's way of the cross. In doing so, she apparently follows a custom common at her time.[23] A very similar scheme is found, for example, in the work of Stephen of Sawley, the early thirteenth century cistercian writer.[24] St Gertrud details the stages of Christ's passion as follows:

Lauds: the royal hostage is seized;
Prime: Jesus is dragged to judgment and sentenced to death;
Terce: Jesus is crowned with thorns;

---

23. Cf. Hart, 145 and ExspSCh, 49.
24. Cf. Stephen of Sawley, 'A Meditation on the Life and Passion of Christ', in 'On the Recitation of the Divine Office', in *Treatises*, CF 36, trans. Jeremiah F. O'Sullivan, ed. Bede K. Lackner (Kalamazoo, 1984) 172–184.

Sext: the blameless man, a spectacle of abuse, is condemned to die on the cross;

None: Jesus breathes out his Spirit for our redemption;

Vespers: Jesus pays the price of his own blood for our salvation;

Compline: Jesus is buried under the seal of the grave, resting in the sleep of love.

In these gradually developed meditations on the salvation mystery, the underlying theme for each of the seven stages remains that Christ's death has given life to us. And while the suffering of Jesus serves as a visual starting point, so to speak, the gist of each meditation lies in our response to Christ's redemption.

Throughout this last chapter, Gertrud relies heavily on allegory. Following the taste of her time, she presents personifications, such as Love, Peace, Wisdom, Charity, and Perseverance. This allegorizing of divine attributes could have a somewhat precious or stifling effect on today's reader were it not for the fact that each one of these allegories represents aspects of the divinity as feminine—a feature of medieval spiritual prose that is of great concern among many Christians today.

The book closes with an image typical of its author and, no doubt, a reference to Gertrud's mystical experience (described in Book Two of the *Legatus*). St Gertrud prays that 'the thornbush of my heart may be converted into . . . a red berry bush of total perfection' (VII, 692f.).

Readers of the *Exercitia* have reason to believe that Gertrud the Great of Helfta achieved this perfect love as far as is humanly possible. They may note, moreover, that what distinguishes this mystic from other women saints (canonized or uncanonized) is St Gertrud's conscious and joyous celebration of her womanhood in Christ.

G. J. L.

Laurentian University
Sudbury, Ontario

SPIRITUAL EXERCISES

I

REBIRTH[1]

TO BE IN THE CONDITION, at the end of your life, of presenting
to the Lord the spotless garment of your baptismal innocence
and the whole and undefiled seal of your christian faith, be
zealous at certain times, especially at Pasch[2] and at Pentecost, in
celebrating the memory[3] of your baptism. Accordingly, desire to be   5
reborn[4] in God through the holiness of new life and to be restored
to a new infancy, and say:

May God be merciful to me and bless me; may his countenance
enlighten me and may he be merciful to me.[5] Let my heart bless him
in all sincerity and truth. Let the ground of my heart quake[6] before
the face of the Lord; let my spirit be recreated and newly remade[7] in   10

---

1. 'Exercise to Restore Baptismal Innocence'.—Our text does not translate the titles (mostly
referring to liturgies) that other editors have provided. We felt these titles would unduly limit
Gertrud's intention. Instead, we have substituted more general headings to point to what we
understand as Gertrud's underlying themes. The missing title translations are provided in footnotes.

2. We have kept the now largely archaic form 'Pasch' instead of altering the word to Easter
or providing a phrase such as Paschal festivities, in order to echo the Latin faithfully: *Pascha et
Pentecoste.*

3. The repetitive use in this text (cf. also II, 1f.;VI, 6) of the phrase 'celebrate the memory
of', which is taken from liturgical language. . . . *in mei memoriam facietis*, concludes the consecration at mass. It is followed by *Unde et memores* in the eucharistic canon. It is also possible,
as the ExspSCh editor suggests, (56, n. 2) that Gertrud had a specific mass text in mind, i.e. that
of the offertory of the Friday after Easter which reads: 'This day shall be a memorial feast for
you and you shall celebrate it as a solemn feast'. Maryknoll Missal (New York 1956). Furthermore, the eucharist itself is often referred to as an *anamnesis* or a celebration of the memory of
Christ. (Cf. LThK 4 (1960 repr. 1986) col. 571.

4. Cf. Jn 3:5.

5. Ps 66:2 (67:1).

6. Ps 113 (114):7.

7. Ps 103 (104):30.

the Spirit of his mouth so that his good Spirit may lead me onto the
right ground.[8]

Then read the symbol of faith—that is, 'I believe in God'—praying to the Lord to make you renounce Satan perfectly and to keep
15   you in the faith that is upright, living, and whole, to the very end of
your life.

Prayer: Lord God, lovingly-kind and true, my creator and redeemer, you have marked me with the holy light of your countenance,[9] you have redeemed me at the dear cost of the blood of your
20   Only Begotten, and, through baptism, you have regenerated me
with the hope[10] of life in the virtue of your Spirit. Make me, with a
true, perfect and whole heart, effectively renounce Satan and all his
pomp and his works. And, by the efficacy of the Holy Spirit, make
me faithfully believe in you, God, my creator, through your Son
Jesus Christ (who is the Way, the Truth, and the Life[11]) with an
25   upright and fervid faith crowned by living works. Make me cling to
you and unyieldingly persevere with you to the very end. Amen.

For the sign of your faith, say:

Holy Trinity, Father, Son, and Holy Spirit, may your divine al-
30   mightiness rule and embolden, your divine wisdom instruct and enlighten, and your divine goodness aid and perfect my faith, so that I
may return it spotless and whole before your face at the hour of
death, together with much interest and the earnings of all my virtues.

35   For the exorcism, pray to the Lord that, by the virtue of his
name, he make you prudently conquer and understand all of Satan's
wiles so that the enemy may never rejoice at overpowering you, but
may withdraw, overcome in every temptation and confounded at
the first encounter.

---

8. Ps 142 (143):10.
9. Ps 4:7 (6).
10. Cf. 1 P 1:3.
11. Jn 14:6.

Prayer: Lord Jesus Christ, great pontiff, who by your precious 40
death have given me life, by the virtue[12] of your Spirit blow away
from me all the crafty devices of the enemy through the efficacy of
your presence. Burst asunder in me all of Satan's snares and, regardful of your compassion, put far from me all blindness of heart.
Christ, may your perfect charity make me triumph viriliously[13] over 45
every temptation. May your holy humility teach me prudently to
shun all snares of the enemy. May your luminous truth lead me and
make me walk in your presence sincerely, with a perfect heart. And
may the blessing of your most indulgent mercy come before and follow after and guard me until the very end of my life. Amen. 50

With these words you will sign yourself with the sign of the holy
cross on your forehead and on your breast:
In the name of the Father and the Son and the Holy Spirit. From
you, O my crucified love, most dulcet Jesus, let me receive the sign 55
of your holy cross on my forehead as in my heart so that I may live
under your protection for eternity. Give me a living faith in your
heavenly precepts so that I may run the way of your commandments[14] with heart wide open. Through you let my conduct be
such that I deserve to become the temple of God and the dwelling
place of the Holy Spirit. Amen. 60

At this point, plead that the highest priest himself, the Lord Jesus,
lay his hand[15] on you so that you may live for eternity in the aid of

---

12. We have chosen to use 'virtue' both in the sense of 'power' and of 'virtue' throughout.
In Gertrud's text *in virtute* overlaps importantly with *efficacia*. The two terms are paralleled
here, as is the case in IV, 52. Cf. also ExspSCh, 58, n. 6.

13. *Viriliter* literally means 'manly'. We have revived the obsolete 'viriliously' to stay in
touch with connections among several words—*vir* (man), *viriliter*, *virtus* (virtue), *virgo* (virgin).

14. Ps 118 (119):32— This passage is also quoted in RB (Prologue 49). The verb *currere* (run)
may derive, as RB suggests, from 2 Tm 4:7. (Cf. also ExspSCh, 62, n. 1). In Gertrud's text,
variations on the wide-open of the heart are repeated in VI, 78, 491, 524, and 704.

15. The biblical synecdoche of the hand or finger of God (and in this text also of Christ) is
used frequently by Gertrud.

the most high and that you may remain under the protection of the
God of heaven.[16]

Under the shadow of your hand[17], most loving Jesus, protect me;
65   let your right hand uphold me.[18] Open the door of your loving-
kindness to me so that, inspired by the sign of your wisdom, I may
truly abstain from every earthly yearning and, glad at the pleasant
scent[19] of your precepts, serve you gladly in your holy church and
progress from day to day, from virtue to virtue.[20] Amen.

70   That God may give you an angel as guide on your road, [say]:

Ah, Jesus, prince of peace[21] and angel of great counsel, may you
yourself always be the guide at my right and the guardian of my pilgrimage,[22] lest I move away and stray from you. And deign to send
from heaven your holy angel,[23] who, under your lovingly-kind care,
75   will be solicitous for me and, according to your gracious purpose,
direct me and lead me, perfect, along your way back to you. Amen.

To greet and receive the angel, [say]:

Greetings, holy angel of God, guardian of my soul and body.
Through the most dulcet heart of Jesus Christ, the Son of God, for

---

16. Ps 90 (91):1.

17. Is 49:2.

18. Ps 17:36 (18:35).

19. This phrase (literally 'sweet scent, odor') is part of the vocabulary of what has been called
the spiritual senses, which uses sense experience as analogies to mystical states. Another example in this chapter is *aures cordis tui* (the ears of your heart) (I, 96) (also in RB Prol. 1). While
sight and hearing seem to cause few if any problems, the use of taste, smell and touch for
spiritual analogies (even though found in the Bible) is likely to seem strange to the modern
reader. Gertrud's use of the spiritual senses is evident throughout, but especially cf. IV, 410ff.,
V, 468ff. and VII, 595ff. Cf. Pierre Doyère, 'Sainte Gertrude et les sens spirituels', *RAM* 144
(1960) 429–446; and Pierre Doyère, 'Les Sens spirituels' in *Legatus* (143) 359–366. In general:
Mary Anita Ewer, *A Survey of Mystical Symbolism* (London/New York 1933) ch. 3 and appen-
dix B; Fridolin Marxer, *Die inneren geistlichen Sinne* (Freiburg/Basel/Vienna 1963) esp. 51–79
re. the tradition on the spiritual senses in the mystical works from Origen to Ignatius of Loyola.

20. Ps 83:8 (84:7).

21. Is 9:6.

22. The terms *peregrinatio* (pilgrimage), *via* (way), and *iter* (road), *exilium* (exile) and *incolatus*
(which has basically the same meaning as 'exile' and which we translated as 'sojourn') carry the
biblical theme of life on earth as transitory. Compare also a number of passages in Bernard,
e.g., SC 24:3.

23. Cf. Ex 23:20.

love of him who created you and me, for love of him who com-   80
mended me to you at baptism, take me into your most faithful
fatherly care. May I, then, aided by you, pass through the torrent of
this life along a spotless path until, with you, I come gladly to see
that mellifluous face which you see: that merriest radiance of impe-   85
rial divinity, dulcet beyond all sweetness.

At this point, you will pray that your mouth be filled with the salt
of wisdom that you may be able to savor the taste of faith in the
Holy Spirit:

Most dulcet Jesus, let me receive from you the salt of wisdom and
the spirit of understanding favorable to eternal life. Amen.   90

Prayer: Make me taste the pleasantness of your Spirit; make me
hunger for your will; make me know your gracious purpose that my
service may always be acceptable to you. Amen.

And so, signing your ears and nose with the sign of the holy cross,   95
you will pray to the Lord that he himself open wide the ears of your
heart to his law[24] and fill all that is within you[25] with the scent of his
fame.[26]

Ah Jesus, shepherd very close to my heart, make me, an unworthy little sheep, always follow and acknowledge your most   100
dulcet voice;[27] and, by the most pleasant scent of living faith, make
me run to pastures of eternal life, where I can be at leisure[28] for eternity and see that you, my Lord, are truly pleasant.[29]

---

24. 2 M 1:4-5.
25. According to ExspSCh, 65, n. 7, this phrase may have been taken from Will iam of Saint
Thierry, *On Contemplating God,* CF 3. Trans. Sr. Penelope Lawson (Kalamazoo 1977) 38.3,
where the translation for *omnia interiora mea* appears as 'my whole being'. —For Williams's influence on Gertrud, see also ExspSCh, 77, n. 5.
26. 2 Co 2:14.
27. Cf. Jn 10:27.
28. The Latin *vacare* is repeatedly used in mystical literature to refer to peaceful contemplation, and implies 'leisure devoted to God'. *Vacare* occurs also in: V, 1, 353, 464; VI, 2, 58, and
520. In the passage above, as well as in VI, 58 and 520, *vacare* and *videre* (to see) are combined,
as is, for instance, the case in Ps 45:11 (46:10): 'Pause a while and know that I am God'. For a
discussion of the difference between 'being at leisure'; and 'being idle', cf. William of Saint
Thierry's *Golden Epistle,* CF 12. I.xxi. And cf. also ExspSCh, 156, n. 1.
29. Ps 33:9 (34:8).

On receiving the standard of the salvation-bringing cross in your
105 right hand to enable you to conquer the foe, say:
Most loving Jesus, place the sign of your holy cross in my right
hand; thus walled round by your help, may I always march under
this sign, with my hand armed against all crafty devices of the
enemy. Amen.

110 *Conclusion:* May the almightiness of God the Father bless me.
May the wisdom of the Son bless me. May the most gracious
charity of the Holy Spirit bless me and protect me for eternal life.
Amen.

Afterward, you will pray to the Virgin Mother that she obtain for
115 you a perfect renewal of life, and that, by this grace, she herself, the
venerable rose, become your mother and godmother in such a way
that you may be her true daughter in conduct. And pray that this
very gem of decency may envelop your soul in the mantle of her
cleanliness, preserving you without any spot under her most dulcet
120 tutelage for her Son, the Lord king.[30] And pray that your name
may be numbered among Israel, the choicest lot, so that you have a
share with those who walk in innocence of heart,[31] always seeing
the Lord before them in all of their ways.[32]
Greetings, Mary, queen of clemency,[33] olive tree of mercy,
through whom life's remedy has come to us, queen of clemency.
125 [Greetings,] Virgin Mother of the divine offspring, through whom
the child of supernal light came to us, the scented offspring of Israel.
Ah! Just as you became the true mother of us all through your Son,

---

30. God (Christ) as king is one of the biblical images frequently used in Gertrud's works.
While kingship in this spiritual context is understood in the biblical sense 'Mine is not a
kingdom of this world' (Jn 18:36), the glamor of royalty and the splendor of the imperial en-
tourage are very much part of this image. The fact that, historically speaking, the power of the
medieval monarchs was already much in decline by Gertrud's day reconfirms the impression
that this writer is inspired more by Scripture than by her own life experiences.

31. Ps 100 (101):2.

32. Ps 15 (16):8

33. The key terms used in this paragraph suggest a close similarity to the *Salve Regina*, the
antiphon to Mary sung daily in cistercian monasteries as the final chant at compline.

who himself, your one and only Son, did not scorn to become our
brother, now then, for the sake of his love take me, an unworthy
woman,[34] into your motherly care. Aid my faith, keep and instruct   130
it, and become so much the godmother of my renewal and faith
now that you may be my only mother and closest to my heart for
eternity, always caring for me with loving-kindness in this life and
taking me into your full motherliness at the hour of death. Amen.

For giving a name, [say]:   135
Most dulcet Jesus, write my name beneath your mellifluous name
in the book of life. Say to my soul: you are mine; I, your salvation,
have recognized you. No longer are you to be called Forsaken, but
you shall be called My Pleasure in her[35]; let my portion be with you
forever in the land of the living.[36]   140

For immersion in the fountain, [say]:
In the name of the Father and the Son and the Holy Spirit. Ah
Jesus, fountain of life,[37] make me drink a cup of the living water[38]
from you so that, having tasted you, I thirst for eternity for nothing
other than you. Immerse me totally in the depth of your mercy.   145
Baptize me in the spotlessness of your precious death. Make me
new in the blood by which you have redeemed me. In the water
from your holiest side, wash away every spot with which I have
ever spotted my baptismal innocence. Fill me with your Spirit and
possess me totally in purity of body and soul. Amen.   150

For oiling with chrism,[39] pray to the Lord so that the anointing of
his Spirit may teach you all things.[40]

---

34. The Latin reads *me indignam*, 'the unworthy one' in the feminine gender. We have
throughout attempted to clarify this female perspective. Simultaneously, on the few occasions
when Gertrud uses a singular masculine gender ending, we have inserted 'man'.

35. Is 62:4.

36. Ps 141 (142):6.

37. Ps 35:10 (36:9).

38. Jn 4:10.

39. The sacramental use of chrism may go back as far as the second century church. Cf.
Liturgie-Lexikon, cols 262ff.

40. 1 Jn 2:27.

155   Holy Father, who through your Son, our Lord Jesus Christ, have
regenerated me by water and the Holy Spirit, give me this day full
remission of all my sins and deign to anoint me with the chrism of
your Spirit for eternal life. Amen. May your peace be with me for
eternity. Amen.

At this point, make the sign of the holy cross on your breast and
your shoulders and say:

160   For the love of your love, make me always bear the pleasant yoke
and the light burden[41] of your precepts on my shoulders and forever
wear the mystery of the sacred faith on my breast like a bunch of
myrrh.[42] Thus, may you remain crucified for me, always fixed
within my heart. Amen.

165   For the white robe, say:

Ah Jesus, sun of justice, make me clothe myself with you[43] so that
I may be able to live according to you[r will]. Make me, under your
guidance, preserve my robe of baptismal innocence white, holy, and
spotless, and present it undefiled before your tribunal, so that I may
have it for eternal life. Amen.

170   In receiving the light, you will pray for inner enlightenment.

Ah Jesus, inextinguishable light, kindle the burning lamp of your
charity within me inextinguishably, and teach me to guard my bap-
175   tism without blame. Then, when called, I come to your nuptials,[44]
being prepared I may deserve to enter into the delights of eternal life
to see you, the true light,[45] and the mellifluous face of your divinity.
Amen.

For receiving communion[46] of the life-giving body and the blood
of the spotless Lamb, Jesus Christ, [say]:

---

41. Mt 11:30.
42. Sg 1:13—Cf. Bernard, SC 43:1: *non fascem, sed fasciculum* (bunch, not bundle).
43. Rm 13:14.
44. Mt 22:3f.; Cf. Rv 19:7.
45. Cf. Ps 35:10 (36:9).
46. Devotion to the eucharist may be seen as 'the most prominent characteristically female concern in the thirteenth-century religiosity'. Cf. Caroline Walker Bynum, 'Women Mystics and the Eucharistic Devotion in the Thirteenth Century', *Women's Studies* 11 (1984) 179–214.

My Lord Jesus Christ, may your venerable body and your   180
precious blood guard my body and my soul for eternal life. Amen.
May your peace be with me. In you, O Jesus, true peace, may I
have peace upon peace eternally, and through you may I come to
that peace[47] which surpasses all understanding[48]—there where, in
gladness, I may see you in yourself for eternity. Amen.   185

In this communion, desire that all your life may be hidden with
Christ in God[49] and that you be found fully consummated at the
hour of death.

O most dulcet guest of my soul, my Jesus very close to my heart,
let your pleasant embodiment[50] be for me today   190
   the remission of all my sins,
   and amends[51] for all my thoughtlessness,
   and also the recovery of all my wasted life.
Let it be for me
   eternal salvation,
   the healing of soul and body,
   the inflaming of love,
   the replenishing of virtue,
   and the enclosing of my life sempiternally in you.   195
Let it be for me
   freedom of spirit,[52]
   health of life,
   honorableness of conduct.

---

47. Peace is 'one of the goals of monastic life'. Cf. RB (Prol. 17), based on Ps 33 (34): 14-15.

48. Ph 4:7—The original Latin (repeated in V, 133 and VII, 141) reads: *quae exsuperat omnem sensum*; it literally means 'which surpasses all senses' and is an allusion to the spiritual senses.

49. Col 3:3.

50. *Incorporatio* is a term used by St Gertrud meaning the joining of two bodies (the blending of one body into another) at the time of communion. Cf. also ExspSCh, 73 n. 4.

51. *Suppletio* (to make amends) is one of Gertrud's (and other medieval mystics') key terms. Cf., e.g., Cyprian Vagaggini, 'The Example of a Mystic: St. Gertrude and Liturgical Spirituality', in C. V., *Theological Dimensions of the Liturgy* (1st ed., Rome 1957), trans. Leonard J. Doyle and W. A. Jurgens (Collegeville, Minn. 1976) 758f. and 765. -Cf. also ExspSCh, 128, n. 3 and 157, n. 3, where *suppletio* is defined as 'reparation et complément'.

52. Cf. 'Contemplation et Liberté' in *Vocabulaire monastique*, 122-128.

Let it be for me
    the shield of patience,
    the mark of humility,
    the staff of firm trust,
    solace in sadness,
    an aid to perseverance.
Let it be for me
    the armor of faith,
    the oak of hope,
    the perfection of charity,
200   the fulfillment of your commandments,
    the renewal of spirit,
    sanctification in truth,[53]
    and the consummation of all religion.[54]
Let it be for me
    the source of virtues,
    the end of vices,
    the growth of all good,
    and the everlasting covenant of your love
    so that, while I am on this pilgrimage set up in body alone, my
205   memory may always abide in avid thought there where you are, my
best share.[55];
    so that, at the termination of my life when the bitterest shell of this
body has been cast aside, I may come to that most dulcet kernel,
    where, in the new star of your glorified humanity, I may see the
very brightest light of your very outstanding divinity,
210   where the most beautiful rose[56] of your mellifluous face may
refresh me by its imperial radiance,
    where, stripped of the troubles of this life, I may gladly feast for

---

53. Jn 17:17—'Sanctification' is here used in its original sense of 'setting aside for, dedicating to God'. Cf. JB, 185 note m.

54. *Religio* (religion) may be generally understood throughout in the sense of 'religious commitment'. *Religare*, literally 'to bind', conveys that sense.

55. Cf. also III, 296 and IV, 310 where Christ is identified as the 'best share'.

56. 'Rose-colored' (*rosa, roseus*) is used in Gertrud's work as the symbolic color for Christ's human-divine nature. See III, 13 and VI, 222, 237 and 668, as well as *Legatus* III. 15, 1, 25 et al. Cf. also ExspSCh, 63, n. 1.

eternity and exult in the riches of your charity, as the spouse[57] rejoices in the delights of her king. Amen.

For confirmation, [say]:
O most victorious king, Jesus, highest priest, embolden me with   215
your almighty virtue, girding me with the sword of your Spirit,[58]
most mighty, so that, always victorious over the thousand frauds of
Satan, I may have my victory in you.

Conclusion: Lord God, who have made me in such a way as also to
reshape me: Ah! renew your Holy Spirit in my viscera today and   220
list me among your adopted people as the offspring of a new race,
that I may rejoice, with the children of the promise, at having received through grace what I do not have by nature.[59]
Make me   225
    great in faith,
    rejoicing in hope,
    patient in tribulation,
    delighting in your praise,
    fervent in spirit,
    faithfully serving you, Lord God, my true king, and persevering
vigilantly with you to the very end of my life. Thus, what I now
believe in hope, I may gladly see with my eyes in reality. Let me see
you as you are; let me see you face to face.[60] There, dear Jesus,   230

---

57. Following Metz, 118f., we have translated throughout *sponsa* and *sponsus* as 'spouse', even though this English term lacks gender identification. For specific distinctions see the Word Index.

58. Eph 6:17; Ps 44:4 (45:3).

59. This phrase (and see III, 24f.) may allude to RB (Prol. 41): 'What is not possible to us by nature, let us ask the Lord to supply by the help of his grace'. A similar passage occurs in William of Saint Thierry: 'man becomes through grace what God is by nature' (*Golden Epistle* II. xvi, 263). ExspSCh, 94, n. 3 refers, in addition, to St Augustine and Pseudo Anselm.

60. 1 Co 13:12.

satiate me with yourself; there, in the fruition[61] of your mellifluous countenance, let there be rest for me forever. Amen. Amen. Amen.

235   May the faithful God, the true Amen,[62] who does not grow faint, make me thirst fervently for the dear Amen with which he himself affects [the soul]; taste with pleasure the dulcet[63] Amen with which he himself refreshes [the soul]; be consummated in happiness by that saving Amen with which he himself perfects [the soul].

Thus may I, by that efficacy, deserve to experience forever the eternal and delightful Amen. Through it, I believe that after this exile I
240   will see the true Amen himself, Jesus, the Son of God, who alone is sufficient for those who love and who, one with the Father and the Holy Spirit, bestows all good things and does not disdain what he has made.[64] Amen. Amen. Amen.

With this prayer, commit your faith and your baptismal innocence to the Lord.

245   My most dulcet Jesus, preserve my baptismal innocence spotless for me in your most gracious heart's repository, together with the hand-written document[65] of my faith so that, under your faithful

---

61. The Latin *fruitio*, as in other spiritual works of the period, is used in this text to refer to the ultimate joyous fulfillment of all desire and striving. It is frequently, as in this passage, associated with seeing God face to face (see V, 169; VI, 294, 590 and 708). As well, *fruitio* connotes sexual enjoyment and is used in the context of the eternal nuptials that promise ultimate satisfaction (see III, 389; V, 259; VI, 90 and VII, 586). Gertrud uses *fruitio* as an attempt to express the *unio mystica*, as may most clearly be seen in IV, 416 and 418; and V, 130 and 132. And cf. also Théodore Koehler, 'fruitio Dei—II. Moyen age latin', DSp 5 (1964) cols 1552–1561.

62. Cf. Rv 7:12.

63. We have rejected the possibility of translating several terms as 'sweet' or its variants. However right 'sweet' may be for *suavis* or *dulcis* in an individual sentence, its repetition throughout the Exercises would created what we feel would be an untruthful impression of saccharinity. To guard against a cloying sweetness, we have taken these steps: *dulcis* is represented by its English cognate 'dulcet' and *mellifluus* by its cognate 'mellifluous'. *Suavis* has become 'pleasant'.

64. This passage (235ff.) contains seven derivatives of the verb *facere* which cannot fully be rendered into English; an attempt was made with affect, effect, perfect etc.

65. According to ExspSCh, 78, n. 2, this passage is reminiscent of Clement of Alexandria (PG 9, 648) and of St John Chrysostomus who speaks repeatedly of the baptismal contract. Jean Chrysostome, *Huit Catéchèse baptismales*, ed. Antoine Wender. SCh 50 (Paris 1957) II. 17, 21f.

guardianship, I may again present them undefiled at the hour of death. Ah, then, stamp my heart with the seal of your heart so that I may be able to live according to you[r will] and, after this exile, 250 come to you gladly, without hindrance. Amen.

II

SPIRITUAL CONVERSION[1]

A S OFTEN AS, with renewed good resolve, you wish to celebrate the memory of your first conversion (by which you did renounce the world) and to turn your heart with all its force to God, use this exercise, praying to God to make you his

5   own monastery of love[2] and of all the virtues.[3]

[Middle High German]	[Latin]
Ah Jesus, beloved of my heart, I have understood that no spiritual fruit can ever grow well unless it is watered by your Spirit and sprinkled with your flowering love. Ah! Would that you now had mercy on me in	Ah Jesus, most cherished of my heart, since it is certain that no spiritual fruit is able to grow strong unless the dew of your Spirit pours over it and it is nurtured by the vigor of your love, only be so merciful to me,

---

1. 'Exercise of Spiritual Conversion'.

2. The 'monastery of love', or in German the *'Minnekloster'*—allegory (cf. also II, 25) belongs to a variety of images referring to buildings in vernacular medieval texts from the thirteenth century on. Cf. Gerhard Bauer, *Claustrum animae. Untersuchungen zur Geschichte der Metapher vom Herzen als Kloster* (Munich 1973) 1: 160. And also Guerric Couilleau, 'Le Coeur et la Cellule', *Vie spirituelle* 134 (1980) 384–392.

3. The Exsp SCh contains three passages that originally appeared in Middle High German and were translated into Latin for the first edition (1536) by Lanspergius. The Following lines, II, 6–30, represent translations both from the Middle High German (left column) and from Latin (right column). A notable difference is one our translation has not captured: the Middle High German was written in rhyming couplets.

such a way that in your arms I might truly begin to warm up through love. My body and soul shall be your own.

My lover, my lover, give me your blessing; flow out and let me in. From my heart, from my heart I long for you, and I beg you, beloved of my heart, that I may be your own. Ah! That in your living love I may sprout out in a new spirituality like the lilies that enjoy the water and the valley.

At this point, pray to the Virgin Mother to entreat for you:

After God my highest consolation, Mary, ah, you white lily, speak to your dear child on my behalf; speak my word well. Defend my cause faithfully and in a motherly way, as I commend myself to you so that I may be accepted by God in the monastery of love, into the school of the Holy Spirit. For you above all have the power to achieve all this with your beloved Son. Faithful Mother, counsel your daughter well so

then, that you receive me into your arms of love and that you warm me totally by your Spirit. 10
Behold my body and soul: these I surrender into your possession.

My cherished, my cherished one, pour your blessing upon me. Open to me your full pleasantness and lead me in. For with my heart and rational soul I desire you; and I pray to you that you alone may possess me. Ah! I am yours and you are 15 mine. Make me always grow with new fervor of spirit in lively love of you and, by your grace, blossom forth like lilies of the valley by the flowing waters.

At this point, pray to the Virgin Mother to beg for you:

After God my greatest hope, 20 ah, white lily, O most dulcet Mary, speak well of me in the presence of your cherished Son; say an efficacious word for me. Defend my cause faithfully. Accomplish [the objectives of] my vows mercifully. For after Christ I trust in you as my one and only hope. Show yourself outright as my gracious Mother. Make the Lord receive me in the cloister of love, in the 25 school of the Holy Spirit, be-that I may grow well in the fruit of living love and lead my life in full spirituality. Amen.

30

cause you more than all others have power to obtain this from your cherished Son. Faithful Mother, see that your daughter becomes a fruit of ever living love and grows in all holiness and perseveres, moistened by dew from heaven.

At this point, invoke the grace of the Holy Spirit to make you progress in religion.

Come, Holy Spirit, come, O God, love;
fill my heart, which, alas, is empty of all that is good.
Set me on fire to love you.
35   Enlighten me to recognize you.
Draw me [to you] to delight in you.
Affect me to [achieve] thorough fruition of you.

At this point, go out from the world and from everything that is not the dulcet Jesus, your love.

Who, most loving Jesus, will give me wings like a dove?—and I
40   will fly in desire, yearning to rest in you.[4]

At this point, hide in Christ Jesus:

Ah! ah! Bright Jesus, through the love by which God was made human you came to seek and to save what was lost.[5] Enter now into me, O my cherished one, and in turn lead me into you. Hide me in
45   the firmest rock of your fatherly defense. In the cavern[6] of your most gracious heart hide me away from all that is not you, O dearest of all dear ones. And grant that my lot be with the people of Israel and my share with you among the daughters of Jerusalem. Amen.

---

4. Ps 54:7 (55:6).
5. Lk 19:10.
6. Cf. Sg 2:14.

At this point, fall down at the feet of Jesus: 50

Bless me, most loving Jesus, bless me and have mercy on me in the loving-kindness of your most gracious heart. Ah! That my soul may choose to know nothing apart from you and that, disciplined[7] by your grace and instructed by the anointing,[8] I may progress well, passionately, and powerfully in the school of your love.[9] 55

For clothing in the spiritual habit, [say]:

Ah! Holy Father, in the love with which you set a mark upon me with the light of your countenance,[10] grant me that I progress in all holiness and virtue.

Christ Jesus, in the love through which you redeemed me with your own blood, clothe me with the purity of your most innocent 60 life.

Almighty holy Paraclete, in the love with which you have marked me out for you with a spiritual name, grant me

to love you with all my heart,

to cling to you with all my soul,

to expend all my force in your love and service,

to live after your own heart;

and, being prepared by you,

to go, at the hour of death, spotless into your nuptials. 65

Pray to the Virgin Mother herself to be your guide in the religious or any other state of life:

O Mary, Mother of God, very close to my heart, clothe me with the fleece of Jesus, intrinsically the Lamb. May he, foremost love, through you, receive, nourish, possess, rule and perfect me. Amen. 70

---

7. *Disciplina* here implies that a person should lead a disciplined way of life (be a *discipulus* (IV, 128) *I discipula* (V, 295), a disciple) and be transformed through God's discipline. See V 304 and 319; VII 173, 476 and 687. Cf. also RB 19. 1–7.

8. Cf. 1 Jn 2:27.

9. fThe 'school of love' (the text has both *schola amoris* and *schola charitatis*—cf. V, 311f., 318 and 365) is an image that often directly refers to the Cistercian monastery. Cf. Karl-Hubert Fischer, *Zwischen Minne und Gott*, Euroäische Hochschulschriften 1:843 (Frankfurt/Bern/New York 1985) 151.

10. Ps 4:7 (6).

At this point, offer the vow of your chastity to your heavenly spouse:

Ah most dulcet Jesus, I have chosen you above all as the trustworthy lover of my soul, the best partner of my life. My rational soul languishes for you.[11] I offer my heart's love to you; I choose
75 you as my companion and guide. I offer my body and soul to you in service. For I am your own, and you are my own.

Ah! Cement[12] me to you, O true love. I offer you my chastity because you are altogether dulcet and pleasant, my spouse full of delight. I vow obedience to you because your fatherly charity allures
80 me, your loving-kindness and gentleness attract me. In observing your will, I tie myself to you because clinging to you is lovable above everything, cherishing you is exceedingly dulcet and to be wished for. I offer myself to you, O my heart's one and only one, so that
85 hereafter I live for you alone because I have found nothing more dulcet [and] have judged nothing more useful than to be more intimately united with you, my cherished one. Ah! Model my heart after your own heart so that I deserve to be totally changed according to your gracious purpose.

Responsory:[13] For the love of my Lord Jesus Christ I have con-
90 temned the kingdom of this world and all the adornments of this age.[14] It is he whom I have seen, whom I have loved, in whom I have believed, whom I have cherished.

Verse: My heart has belched forth a good word. I speak my works to the king.[15] It is he whom I have seen, whom I have loved, in whom I have believed, whom I have cherished.

---

11. More literally: 'Because of you, I endure the languor of my rational soul'.

12. This passage contains several verbs implying close attachment: *conglutinare* (cement), the alliterating pair *allicere* (allure) and *attrahere* (attract) and later *adhaerere* (cling) and finally *uniri* (to be united).

13. This responsory (taken from the *Pontificale*, 131 f.) is repeated twice, see III, 303 and IV, 299. In *Legatus* IV (255) it is used as a meditative theme (54. 3–6). Hart concludes (175) that the Helfta community favored this text for burials and 'in times of special need'.

14. *Saeculum* is often translated as 'world' in the texts of spiritual writers, and it has, no doubt, the meaning of 'this world' in contrast to the 'next world'. But because Gertrud uses both *mundus* (world) and *saeculum*, as is the case in this passage, we will translate *saeculum* throughout as 'age' in the meaning of 'our time or our life here on earth'. See also V, 99.

15. Ps 44:2 (45:1).

Responsory: True author and guardian of decency, born of the   95
Virgin Mary, you have aroused everyone to the sacred love of chastity. Christ, exemplar,[16] hope, and crown of virgins, preserve me
chaste in mind and body through the intercession of the most blessed   100
Virgin Mother Mary.

Verse: Fountain of life,[17] source of light forever and most blessed
author of all goodness.

Prayer: Almighty God sempiternal, look favorably upon our en-
treaties, and give to us, your women servants (who have come together in this one single charity to honor your name) an upright
faith, unshakable hope, true humility, holy devotion, perfect charity,   105
earnestness and steadfastness and perseverance in good works. And
through the merits and intercessions of all saints grant us that there
may be in our hearts a simple[18] affection,[19] strong patience, clean
and spotless religion,[20] pleasing obedience, peace forever, a pure   110
mind, holy awareness, spiritual compunction, virtue of soul, a spotless life, and an irreproachable consummation so that we, running
viriliously, may deserve to go happily into your kingdom. Amen.

---

16. The term *forma*, found in Ps 44:3 (45:2), (and used four times in Gertrud's text) always
refers to Christ. While other translators often ignore the word, we have used 'exemplar' to
represent the most basic meaning, hoping that it may suggest the notions of model, pattern, ar-
chetype, even Plato's 'idea'. All of these meanings are contained in the Latin term.

17. Ps 35:10 (36:9).

18. The term *simplex* (see also VII, 684) has the meaning of 'undivided' (the opposite of
duplicity) and of 'unity'. It is one of the terms favored to characterize the medieval religious.
Vocabulaire monastique, 31–35.

19. Translators seem to agree that there is no satisfactory English term for the complex notion of *affectus*. Our unsatisfactory choice is 'affection'. It is especially odd, perhaps, in the
passage where *affectus* is attributed to both God and the universe (VI, 192f.). As Jean Leclercq
interprets the term for St Bernard's work, *affectus* is a 'profound and ineffable attachment of an
experiential order . . .' (*Bernard of Clairvaux and the Cistercian Spirit*. CS 16, trans. Claire Lavoie
(Kalamazoo 1976) 45). Or, as Thomas X. Davis states, the meaning of *affectus* in William of
Saint Thierry entails both 'the soul's ascent towards God' and 'the condescending grace of
God'. (William of Saint Thierry, *The Mirror of Faith*, CF 15. Trans. T.X.D. (Kalamazoo 1979)
93–95.

20. Jm 1:27.

III

DEDICATION OF THE SELF[1]

I N THIS WAY, you will celebrate the spiritual matrimony, the
marriage of love, the espousal and coupling of your chaste soul
with Jesus, the heavenly spouse, in the unbreakable bond of
cherishing-love.[2]

The voice of Christ to the soul:

5   Look upon me, my dove,[3] at who I am: I am Jesus, your dulcet
friend. Open to me the penetralia[4] of your heart.

I am, indeed, from the land of angels, an exemplar of radiance.[5]
I am myself the splendor of the divine sun.

---

1. 'Exercise of Espousals and Consecration'. Large parts of this chapter are based, often verbatim, on the ceremony of the Consecration of Virgins (*Pontificale*, 126– 149). Our notes will
draw attention throughout to passages in this liturgy. We also drew comparisons from the
tenth century Pontifical from Germany which the Helfta nuns are likely to have known: *Le
Pontificale Romano-Germanique du dixième siecle* I, Studi e Testi 226 by M. Andrieu. Eds. Cyrille
Vogel and Reinhard Elze (Vatican City 1963).

2. The Latin term here is *dilectio*, distinct from *amor* and *amare* which have appeared as 'love'
up to now. Since there is no adequate synonym for 'love' in English we have used 'cherish' for
the verb *diligere* and the compound 'cherishing-love' for *dilectio* in order to differentiate between
the two Latin words. The third Latin term for love, i.e. *caritas*, has been translated throughout
as 'charity'.

3. Cf. Sg 2:10 and 5:2.

4. We have kept the English equivalent to the Latin *penetralia* in its meaning of 'the innermost parts or recesses' or 'the most private or secret things'.

5. Ps 44:3 (45:2).

I am the most fulgent spring day, the only one that grows ever
bright and knows no waning. The majesty of my superessential   10
glory whose extent is measured only by eternity, fills heaven and
earth. Only I wear on my head the imperial diadem of my glorious
deity. I bear the garland of my rose-colored blood, which I spilled
for you. Neither above nor below the sun is there anything like me.[6]
At the gesture of my hand, lily-white choruses of virgins come forth.   15
And I go before them in the chorus of eternal life, in the delights of
my divinity. I refresh them with the pleasant[7] fruition of spring-like
merriment. Nevertheless, I do not scorn to lower my eyes to the
valley where I can gather violets that are without spots.

Therefore, whichever woman wants to cherish me, [is] the same   20
one whom I want to espouse and to cherish and to love passionately.
I will teach her the song of virgins, which will sound so dulcet from
my throat that she will be compelled to be united with me in the
most pleasant bond of love. What I am by nature she herself will become by grace. I will wind my arms of love around her, drawing her   25
close to the very heart of my deity in order that, by virtue of my
burning love, she will melt like wax before the fire.[8] My beloved
dove, if you want to be mine, you need to cherish me dulcetly,
wisely, and strongly, and to be capable of experiencing all this pleasantly in yourself.

Love arouses the soul: 30
Ah! Wake up, o soul! How long will you sleep? Hear the word
that I announce to you. Above the heavens there is a king who is
held by desire for you. He loves you with his whole heart, and he
loves beyond measure. He himself loves you so dulcetly and he himself cherishes you so faithfully that, for your sake, he humbly gave   35
up his kingdom. Seeking you, he endured being seized as a thief.

---

6. Cf. Ex 15:11

7. We felt that here we had to make an exception to our usual choice of translating *amoenus*
by 'lovely'.

8. Ps 67:3 (68:2). The metaphor of the heart melting like wax near the divine fire is frequently encountered in works of mysticism. Another scriptural base may be Ps 21:15 (22:14) (cf.
Lüers). While Gertrud uses this full image only once, she may be alluding to it with the verbs *li-
quefacere, liquescere* ('melt, become liquid').

He himself loves you so heartily,
cherishes you so vigorously,
is jealous for you so dulcetly,
is zealous for you so powerfully
that, for you, he cheerfully surrendered his flower-like body to
death. This is he who washed you in his blood; who, through his
40   death, set you free. How long will he wait for you to love him in
return?
    He himself bought you and your love at exceeding cost.
    He himself cherished you above his honor.
    He himself loved you more than his noble body which, for your
sake, he never spared. Then he—dulcet love, pleasant charity, faithful lover—exacts from you reciprocal love. If you want to accept it
45   very quickly, he is ready to espouse you. Hurry then to tell him
what you choose.

    The voice of the soul offering itself to God:
    I am an orphan without a mother, needy and poor I am.[9] Except
for Jesus, I have no consolation.
50   Only he himself can quench my soul's thirst.
    He himself is the one chosen above all and the only friend of my
heart.
    He himself is King of kings and Lord of lords.[10]
    If he himself, the supreme ruler, wants to show his clemency to me,
a miserable woman, to me, the vilest woman; if he himself wants to
55   deal with me in his mercy, in his unlimited loving-kindness, in this
his goodness alone prevails, and this depends on his good will. I am
his own. He has my body and soul in his hand. He himself may do
with me whatever seems right to his loving-kindness. Oh, who will
grant me[11] to become a human being after his own heart so that he
60   might have his desire in me equally with his best gracious purpose.
This alone could gladden and console me. Ah Jesus, the one and

---

9. Ps 85 (86): 1. See also VII, 130 for a repetition. And cf. Bernard, SC 1.4.
10. Rv 19:16; 1Tm 6:15.
11. Jb 23:3.

only cherished of my heart, dulcet lover, cherished, cherished, cherished above all that has ever been cherished, for you, O flowering spring day filled with life, the amorous desire of my heart sighs and languishes. Oh, if only it happened to me to become more closely 65 united with you to the end that then the flowers and fruit of my spiritual growth might sprout under you, the true sun. Expectantly, I have waited for you.[12] Come, then, to me like a turtledove to her consort. You have wounded the penetralia of my heart[13] with your radiance and beauty.[14] My cherished, my cherished one, if I am not united with you I will never, for eternity, be able to be glad. Ah 70 friend, friend, friend, fulfill your desire and mine effectively.

Christ's voice:
I will espouse you in my Holy Spirit; I will draw you close in inseparable union with me. You will be my guest, and 75
I will shut you up in my lively cherishing-love,
I will make you a robe of the noble purple of my precious blood;
I will crown you with the choice gold of my bitter death.
I will fill up your desire with myself and thus
I will bring gladness to you forever.

There follows the consecration in which the soul faithful to Christ 80 totally consecrates, offers, and espouses herself to the virile one[15] in order to show herself to Christ as a chaste virgin.[16] In observance of her virginity and chastity she will faithfully cling to the same one, her heavenly spouse, with a pure heart and chaste body, in a unifying love which should not be defiled by cherishing anything created.
And at first, to commend your spouse, recite: 85
Who is like you, my Lord Jesus Christ, my dulcet love, exalted

12. Ps 39:2 (40:1).
13. Sg 4:9.
14. Ps 44:5 (45:4).
15. We have chosen to translate *unus vir* as 'the virile one' in order to bring out the etymological connection between 'virility' and 'virginity' that is exploited in this passage.
16. 2 Co 11:2.

and measureless, you who look upon the humble?[17] Who is like you
in strength, Lord,[18] you who choose the weak of this world?[19] Who
90   is like you who founded heaven and earth, whom thrones and
dominations serve—you who *will* your delight to be with the children of humankind?[20] How great you are, King of kings and Lord
of lords,[21] who rule the stars and set your heart on humankind.[22]
What are you like in whose right hand are riches and glory?[23] Are
95   you filled with delight and have a spouse from earth? O love, how
low do you bend your majesty? Ah! O love, where do you lead the
fountain of wisdom?[24] Surely to the very abyss of misery. O love, to
you alone, to you alone belongs this excellent wine in abundance[25]
by which your divine heart is conquered and intoxicated.

100   Proof of love:
This is our God who cherishes us[26] with unconquerable love,
with inestimable charity, with inseparable cherishing-love;[27] who,
because of this, took on himself the bodily substance of our earth to
become a spouse and take a spouse for himself; who cherished us
105   with his entire being. To love him is to have wed him.

---

17. Cf. Ps 112: (113:7).
18. Ex 15:11.
19. 1 Co 1:27.
20. Pr 8:31.
21. Rv 19:16; 1 Tm 6:15.
22. Jb 7:17.
23. Pr 3:16.
24. Cf. Pr 18:4.
25. Esth 1:7.
26. 1 Jn 4:10—Cf. ExspSCh (100, n. 3) that cites allusions to both William of Saint Thierry
and Bernard of Clairvaux.
27. Gertrud's sequence of love, charity and cherishing-love (*amor, caritas* and *dilectio*) is reminiscent of the steps of love given in William of Saint Thierry's *Golden Epistle*. Cf. 88.225 and
94.257; and see also Déchanet's Introduction, xxv.
26. 1 Jn 4:10—Cf. ExspSCh (100, n. 3) that cites allusions to both William of Saint Thierry
and Bernard of Clairvaux.
27. Gertrud's sequence of love, charity and cherishing-love (*amor, caritas* and *dilectio*) is reminiscent of the steps of love given in William of Saint Thierry's *Golden Epistle*. Cf. 88.225 and
94.257; and see also Déchanet's Introduction, xxv.

Come! Come! Come![28]

I come, I come, I come[29] to you, most loving Jesus, whom I have loved, whom I have sought, whom I have wished for. Because of your gentleness, loving-kindness, and charity, loving you with all my heart, all my soul, and all my virtue, I follow you who call me. 110 Put me not to confusion, but deal with me according to your gentleness, and according to the mulitude of your mercies.[30]

By this litany invoke the help of all the saints:[31]

O fountain of sempiternal lights, holy Trinity! God, by your divine almightiness embolden me by your divine wisdom; rule me by your 115 divine goodness; fashion me after your own heart.

Father of heaven, King of kings,[32] ah! deign to perform in me the nuptials for your Son, the king.

Jesus Christ, Son of the living God, ah! may my love celebrate the nuptials with you, for you are yourself my king and my God. 120

Holy Spirit, Paraclete, ah! with that glue of love with which you unite Father and Son, unite my heart with Jesus forever.

Holy Mary, Mother of the king, of the Lamb, of the spouse of virgins, ah! lead me with clean heart and body into dwelling to- 125 gether with your Son Jesus.

All holy angels and archangels, ah! obtain entrance for me, in angelic purity, into the inner chamber of Jesus, my spouse.

All holy patriarchs and prophets, ah! obtain for me such charity as 130 Jesus, my spouse, requires from me.

---

28. These repetitions represent a liturgical invitatory with response. Cf. also ExspSCh 101, n. 4.

29. This threefold response is an adaptation of the beginning of the Consecration ceremony: *Pontificale*, 127.

30. Dn 3:42.

31. Gertrud again (and IV, 100ff.) follows the basic pattern of a litany but adapts it to her own style. In the Consecration ceremony, the litany is sung while the candidates are lying prostrate before the altar (*Pontificale*, 129).

32. Rv 19:16; 1 Tm 6:15.

All holy apostles, ah! pray that I experience the kiss of his mellifluous mouth,[33] of the living Word of God,[34] which you have touched.

All holy martyrs, ah! obtain for me a desire so forceful that, with
135   the palm of martyrdom, I deserve to go out towards him who wears a garland of roses and lilies.

All holy confessors, ah! obtain for me [the ability] to imitate in all perfection[35] and holiness, the conduct of Jesus, my spouse.

All holy virgins, ah! pray for me, that, with chaste love, I may
140   deserve to build a nest like a turtledove[36] in the wound of love of Jesus, my spouse.

All saints, ah! obtain entrance for me (a woman so worthily prepared) into the nuptials of the Lamb[37], just as each one of you has entered to see the face of God.

Be favorable and fashion me after your own heart, Lord.
145   Be favorable and free me from all that keeps me from you, Lord.

Through your incarnation, make me cherish you dulcetly, wisely, and strongly with all my heart.

Through your passion and death, make me die to myself and live
150   for you alone.

Through your glorious resurrection and wondrous ascension, make me progress day by day from virtue to virtue.[38]
155   At the hour of death, succor me with all the viscera of your mercy and gladden me in joy with your countenance, Lord.[39]

On the day of judgment, do not let my soul fear hearing evil,[40] but make me hear the glory of your voice: Come, blessed ones of my Father![41]

---

33. The kiss of the divine mouth, inspired by Sg 1:1, became the symbol of the mystical union in the bridal imagery of the works of the medieval mystics. Cf. St Bernard, SC 8.
34. Cf. 1 Jn 1:1.
35. Cf. 1 Co 11:1.
36. Cf. Jr 48:28.
37. Rv 19:9.
38. Ps 83:8 (84:7).
39. Ps 20:7 (21:6).
40. Ps 111(112):7.
41. Mt 25:34.

Through her who gave you birth make me, like a true spouse, ex-   160
perience the marriage of your chaste love.

[As] sinners, we beg you to hear us.

Deign to preserve for yourself in me, whole and unimpaired—as
the apple of your eye[42]—the resolve to be chaste that I offer you;
we beg you to hear us.   165

Make me experience in spousal love and in nuptial embrace who
and what you are; we beg you to hear us.

Grant me the betrothal gift[43] of your Spirit with the dowry of
your most whole love: we beg you to hear us.

Make me go on my way to you in my nuptial gown among the   170
sensible virgins and with a kindled lamp at the hour of death as
spouse to spouse[44]: we beg you to hear us.

Lead me as your own, by the kiss of your mellifluous mouth,[45] into
the inner chamber of the festival of your love: we beg you to hear us.   175

Make all of us who are your servants in this place cherish you
wholeheartedly, cling to you inseparably and please you forever
with sincerity of mind and body: we beg you to hear us.

Make us entreat for what you are delighted to heed: we beg you   180
to hear us.

Jesus, Son of the living God, heed us in the efficacy of your divine
love.

Lamb of God, you take away the sins of the world,[46] rid me of all
my sins[47] according to the multitude of your mercies.[48]

Lamb of God, you take away the sins of the world, with your in-   185
extinguishable charity make amends for all my negligence.

---

42. Ps 16(17):8.

43. As she often does, St Gertrud here used two different terms (*arrba* and *dotalium*) for
essentially the same meaning. Moreover, she may have in mind a pun in which *arrba* functions
both as a synonym for marriage dowry (within the bridal context of this passage) and a sum of
money required of a postulant in a convent.

44. Cf. Mt 25:3-6. This passage is sung as the first antiphon during the Consecration
ceremony (*Pontificale*, 126f.).

45. Sg 1:1.

46. Jn 1:29.

47. Cf. Ps 50:3 (51:1).

48. Dn 3:42.

Lamb of God, you take away the sins of the world,[49] release me
in peace at the hour of death in such a way that I may see you face
to face.[50]
Lord have mercy. Christ have mercy. Lord have mercy.[51]

190   *Prayer*: Ah Jesus, my spouse [crowned] with flowers[52]—just as
death carries the soul away from the body, so may your love carry
my heart into you so that I may cling inseparably to you as if by glue.

Verse: Receive[53] me, my Jesus, into the abyss of your mercy, and
wash away every spot from me in the depth of your clemency.
195   Receive me, my Jesus, into the embrace of your co-operation so
that I may deserve to be coupled with you in a contract of perfect
union.

Receive me, my Jesus, into the very pleasant marriage of your love.
There, make me experience the kiss of your mellifluous mouth.

A prayer for perfect chastity of soul and body:[54]
200   God, you graciously inhabit chaste bodies and uncorrupted souls.
God, by your word through whom everything was made, you so

---

49. This threefold repetition of *Agnus Dei* (see also IV, 210ff.) is taken from the prayer
before communion in the liturgy of the mass (used ever since the seventh century). *Liturgie-
Lexikon*, col. 9.

50. 1 Co 13:12.

51. Gertrud's text has *Kyrie eleison. Christe eleison. Kyrie eleison.* Used in Greek at the beginning of the mass liturgy since the sixth century (*Liturgie-Lexikon*, col. 198), it is also a part of the
canonical hours (RB 17.4–10).

52. According to ExspSCh, 106, n. 4, *floridus* may also refer to a wreath of flowers worn by
the spouse in medieval marriage ceremonies. If this is what Gertrud alludes to in this passage, it
may also be associated with the crown of thorns.

53. The threefold repetition of the *Suscipe* (taken from the Consecration ceremony) is already
mentioned in RB 58.21–22. Cf. also ExspSCh, 106, n.5.

54. The following lines (200–258) constitute the entire Preface sung by the bishop during
the Consecration ceremony (see the tenth century Pontifical, 42f. and *Pontificale*, 132–40).
Gertrud quotes the long passage almost word for word. Brief, but in some cases important
changes include adapting the text to the first person singular, inserting the attribute 'unworthy'
in line 208, and most notably changing the phrase *amore te timeant* ('that they may *fear* you
with love') to *amore te diligam* ('with love let me *cherish* you') in line 243.

heal human substance, tainted by devilish fraud in the first human
beings, that you not only recall human nature to the innocence of
its first source but also lead it to the experience of certain goods to   205
be obtained [only] in a new age, and thus advance those still bound
to the condition of mortals to a resemblance with angels. Look
upon me, your unworthy woman servant, who place in your hand
my resolve of self-restraint. I offer my devotion to you from whom
I took the very same vow I offer.   210

For how could the rational soul enclosed in mortal flesh conquer
the law of nature, the freedom of license, the force of habit, and the
urges of youth[55] unless, through [our] free will, you kindled this
love of chastity [and] fed this yearning in our hearts and poured out   215
the strength [for it].[56] For indeed, your grace has been poured over
all peoples from every nation under the sky; heirs of the new covenant (as innumerable as the number of stars) have been adopted.
Among other virtues that you imparted to your children—born not
of blood nor of the will of the flesh but of your Spirit[57]—this gift also   220
has flowed into certain minds from the fountain of your bounty. And
while esteem for nuptials is not diminished by any interdiction, and
while the original blessing abides with holy wedlock, there are,
nevertheless, sublimer souls who despise the coupling of man and
woman in marriage. They yearn for the sacrament but cherish only   225
what is prefigured [therein] and do not imitate what happens in the
nuptials.

Blessed virginity has known her author well, and in emulation of
angelic wholeness, has devoted herself to his inner chamber, to the
bedchamber of him who is forever the Son of virginity just as he is   230
forever the spouse of virginity. Then, Lord, give to me, who im-
plore you for help and yearn to be emboldened by the sacrament of
your blessing, the defence and direction of your protection, lest the
ancient foe (who undermines [my] loftier zeal with subtler crafty
devices) creep in through some carelessness of mind to darken the   235

---

55. *Aetas* literally means 'age'.
56. *Fortitudo*, 'courage' or 'strength', as we have translated throughout, is one of the cardinal
virtues.
57. Jn 1:13.

palm of perfect self-restraint and rob me of the resolve to be chaste,
which is becoming even to the conduct of widows.[58]
Let there be in me, Lord, through the gift of your Spirit,
    prudent modesty,
240   wise graciousness,
    grave leniency,
    chaste freedom.
Let me be fervent in charity, let me cherish nothing apart from you,
let me live praiseworthily without striving for praise. Let me glorify
you in holiness of body [and] in purity of soul. With love let me
cherish you; with love let me serve you.

    Be you my honor,
    you my joy,
    you my voluptuousness,
245   you my consolation in sorrow,
    you my counsel in uncertainty,
    you my defense in injustice,
    my patience in tribulation,
    my abundance in poverty,
    my food in fasting,
    my sleep in wakefulness,
    my remedy in weakness.

Let me have everything in you, whom I earnestly strive to love
250 above everything; and let me guard what I have professed. Scruti-
nizer of hearts, let me be pleasing to you, not in body but in mind.
Let me pass over to the number of wise maidens to wait for my
heavenly spouse with a kindled lamp and with the oil of prepared-
ness. And let me not be troubled by the unforeseen arrival of the
king; but let me, secure with my light, run up to meet him gladly in
255 the chorus of the virgins who go before him. And let me not be shut
out with the foolish virgins, but permit me to go into the royal

---

58. In line 237, which is a change from the Pontifical (cf. also ExspSCh, 110, n. 2), St Gertrud talks about the three stations in life for women, established in patristic literature: virgins,
married women, and widows. Cf. Matthäus Bernards, *Speculum virginum, Geistigkeit und
Seelenleben der Frau im Hochmittelalter*, Forschungen zur Volkskunde 36/38 (Cologne 1955)
40–53.

palace with the wise ones. And let me abide in chastity, to remain forever among the followers of your Lamb. [This I ask] through the same Lord.[59]

On spiritually receiving the veil, say:

Responsory: The Lord has clothed me with the garment of sal-   260
vation and enclosed me in the clothing of gladness. And, like a
spouse, he has made me comely with a crown.

Verse: The Lord has clothed me with a stately robe woven in gold
and has adorned me with priceless necklaces. And, like a spouse, he
has made me comely with a crown.[60]

Prayer: Ah, O my cherished one, chosen out of thousands, make   265
me rest under the shadow of your charity, and cover me all around
with the fleece of your spotlessness. There from your hand I will accept the veil of cleanliness which, under your direction and guidance, I will submit untorn before the tribunal of your glory with the
fruit of most innocent chastity increased a hundredfold.   270

On putting on the crown,[61] [say]:

Antiphon: He placed the sign on my face so that I might admit no
other lover but himself.

---

59. The phrase *Per eundem Dominum* (which we translated by adding a phrase from today's vernacular liturgy) is a traditional closing of liturgical prayers that are supposed to be directed to the Father by way of mediation through Christ, as stated in Rm 1:8, Heb 13:15, 1Pt 2:5, and elsewhere. Cf. *Liturgie-Lexikon*, cols 78f.

60. Lines 260–264 are already found in the tenth century Pontifical (44) and in the Office of St Agnes (cf. ExspSCh, 113, n. 2 and Hart, 177). Lines 260f. are, moreover, discussed in *Legatus* III (143) 30. 19.

61. The crown (see also III, 335), and the ring (see III, 288f. and 297), have functioned as symbols in the consecration of virgins; they were taken directly from marriage ceremonies where they had been used since the tenth century. The ring, in fact, goes back to Teutonic times as a symbol of betrothal. Cf. René Metz, 'La Couronne et l'Anneau dans la consécration des vierges. Origine et évolution des deux rites dans la liturgie latine', *Revue des sciences religieuses* 28 (1954) 113–132 and repr. in: R.M., *La Femme et l'Enfant dans le droit canonique médiéval* (London 1985) chapter vii.

Responsory: I love Christ into whose inner chamber I have gone,
275   whose Mother is a virgin, and whose Father knows no wife,[62]
whose vocal organ[63] sings to me with melodious voices.
When I love him I am chaste.
When I touch him I am clean.
280   When I receive him I am a virgin.

Verse: I have received honey and milk from his mouth, and his
blood has adorned my cheeks.[64]
When I love him I am chaste,
When I touch him I am clean,
When I receive him I am a virgin.

Prayer: Ah! O my brother[65] and spouse Jesus, great king, God and
Lamb! Place, place such a sign on the face of my soul that I may
choose nothing, yearn for nothing, and cherish nothing but you
under the sun. And you yourself, O dearest of all dear ones, deign
285   so to be coupled to me in the contract of sacramental matrimony
that for you I may become a true spouse and wife through an inseparable love, stronger than death.[66]

---

62. This passage appears verbatim in the text ascribed to the Augsburg recluse Engelbirn,
who wrote or translated presumably in the first half of the thirteenth century. The Engelbirn
text reads in the original Middle High German as follows:

ich minne den heiligen Krist,
in des brutbette ich bin gegangen,
des muter ein mait ist,
unde sin vater kennet niht wibes.

(Ms. Munich Cgm 94, reprinted in Eduard Gebele, 'Engelbirn von Augsburg', *Lebensbilder aus
dem Bayerischen Schwaben* 8 (1961) 62.) The common source for both Gertrud's text (lines 275
to 280) and Engelbirn's text is St Ambrose's 'Vita S. Agnetis' in *Bollandus Acta Sanctorum*
(Paris) Jan. 11 col. 714.

63. *Organum* could be translated as 'musical instrument'. But Gertrud's contexts reveal that
she has in mind the human musical instrument, thereby making, in effect, *organum* and *vox*
duplicates. Our translation attempts to follow Gertrud in giving these words separate forms but
nearly identical meaning.

64. From the Consecration ceremony, sung after communion. *Pontificale*, 148.

65. Cf. Sg 8:1.

66. Cf. Sg 8:6.

For the ring, [say]:

Antiphon: He has given me his ring[67] as a pledge,[68] he who is far
nobler than all human beings both in birth and worthiness.   290

Responsory: Already his body is in companionship with my body,
and his blood has adorned my cheeks, he whose Mother is a virgin,
whose Father knows no wife.

Verse: I am espoused to him whom the angels serve and at whose
beauty sun and moon marvel.[69]

Prayer: Ah my Jesus, fruit and flower of a virgin's decency, best   295
share of my inheritance, and royal dowry, who have given me the
ring of faith as a pledge, the seal of your Spirit; make me suited to
you, my living lily, loveliest flower.[70] Join me so indissolubly to that
most burning love of yours that, by force of how I cherish being
with you, I may thirst for death. And let the contract which you   300
entered into with me transport my heart away from me so that
from now on it may not be with me any more but may live with
you in undivided love.

Responsory: For the love of my Lord Jesus Christ I have contemned the kingdom of this world and all the adornments of this
age. It is he whom I have seen, whom I have loved, in whom I have   305
believed, whom I have cherished.

Verse: My heart has belched forth a good word; I speak my works
to the king,[71] whom I have seen, whom I have loved, in whom I
have believed, whom I have cherished.

Prayer:[72] Grant, we seek, almighty God, that I, your unworthy
woman servant, who desire to be consecrated to you, Lord, in the   310

---

67. *Legatus* III (143) 2. 1 devotes a chapter to the meaning of 'the rings of spiritual espousal'.

68. See *Pontificale*, 142f.

69. See the tenth century Pontifical, 39.

70. In this and a number of cases, we have accepted an unwanted alliteration for the sake of
consistency of vocabulary. For the same reason, we have sometimes had to do without Gertrud's frequent alliterations.

71. Ps 44:2 (45:1).

72. Lines 308–316, which Gertrud adapted to the first person singular simultaneously inserting 'unworthy', are found in the tenth century Pontifical (44). And cf. also Metz, 204 n. 150
and Hart, 178.

woman servant, who desire to be consecrated to you, Lord, in the hope of eternal reward, may abide in my holy resolve in full faith and with my rational soul steadfast. You, almighty Father, deign to sanctify, bless, and consecrate me forever. Bestow on me humility, chastity, obedience, charity, and a great quantity of all good works.

315   Grant me, Lord, glory for my works, reverence for my shamefastness, and holiness for my decency so that I may be capable, together with your holy angels, of praising your most glorious worthiness for eternity. Amen.

For the episcopal blessing, demand[73] that you be blessed by all the imperial Trinity:

320   May the dulcet fatherliness of God the Father and his majestic divinity bless me and co-operate with me. May the dulcet affinity and the consanguinity in human propinquity of Jesus Christ, God, bless me and couple me to him. May the dulcet graciousness of the Holy Spirit and his fiery charity bless me and make me fertile. May all the

325   imperial Trinity bless, embolden, and invigorate me.

May the glorious humanity of Jesus Christ, God, bless and unite me closely with him who deigned to choose me for himself from this world, demonstrating through his death how much he cherished me, and who wed me to his love. Thus, by his saving, living, and most dulcet blessing, may I seize the perfection of all virtues,

330   guard the whole and spotless chastity that I have professed, keep [my] resolve, show humility, cherish chastity, preserve patience, and persevere in all holiness until the very end. And after this life, may I

335   deserve to receive the crown of chastity—in a long white gown among the lily-like band following you, Lamb without spot, Son of the Virgin Mary—wherever you go, flower of virgins.[74] Amen.

---

73. St Gertrud uses 'demand' (*postulare*) three times in the *Exercitia* (cf. V, 405 and VI, 768). Her language, even in prayer, may seem to be at times harsh and impatient (cf. also, for instance, VI, 52f.).

74. Rv 14:4–5.

At this point, pray that the lovingly-kind Lord re-entrust you into
the keeping of his lily-like Mother, the Virgin Mary (in lieu of the
abbess) to be received again from her hand.[75]   340

O cherished one of my vows, O Jesus, dearest of all the dearest
ones, re-entrust and recommend me now to your Mother, the imperial virgin rose, to be forever, for the sake of your love, the guide
and custodian of my virginity. Entrust me to those tender hands
that nourished and reared you, Son of God the Father, that they   345
may defend and aid my resolve to be chaste, leading me without
spot along the way of virginal cleanliness and a nun's self-restraint.
Ah! ah! Please, say to this virginal rose on my behalf: 'Receive her
into your motherly care; I commend her to you in the total virtue   350
of my divine charity. See to it, Mother, that you present her again
spotless and re-entrust her to me reared after my own heart'. Amen.

For the hymn, 'We praise you, God', sing your praise of the al-
ways-venerable Trinity with this prayer: 355

Holy Trinity, from which there shines forth the living deity,
[from which] there distill life, love, and *sophia*, [from which] there
wells forth innate virtue, co-essential wisdom, overflowing pleasantness, fiery charity, extensive holiness, all encompassing goodness—
to you praise, honor and glory; to you thanksgiving, power, and   360
bright homage because you, high cedar of Lebanon, extending
above the cherubs with the royal majesty of divinity, are, in this
abysmal valley of misery, delighted to be joined with this twig of
hyssop in a nuptial embrace, in spousal love. And you, O God, love
(the nexus and friendship of the Holy Trinity) recumbent you   365
repose and take delight among the children of humankind in holy
decency, which, through your loving virtue, blazes up in your holy
delights, like a rose gathered among thorns.

O love, love, where does one go for such loveliness? Where does

---

75. St Gertrud adapts a rubric from the Consecration ceremony where the bishop
presented the young nuns to their abbess. *Pontificale*, 149.

one come to such fatness[76] of spirit? Where, where is the way of life
370   leading to the meadows whose dew is God,[77] refreshing thirsting
hearts? O love, you alone know this road of life and truth.
In you are carried out dear contracts with the Holy Trinity.
Through you are dispensed the higher charismata of the Spirit.[78]
From you overflow the more plentiful seeds of the fruits of life.
Out of you wells forth the sweeter honey of the delights of God.
375   From you pour out the fatter drops of the blessings of the Lord of
hosts—those dear pledges of the Spirit which are, alas alas, exceedingly uncommon in our land.
O love, O love, in your beautiful cherishing-love, prepare my way
380   to you. In chaste charity let me follow you forever. In the love of
the nuptial contract, [let me follow] where you reign and govern in
the fullest majesty of your divinity, [where] in the most dulcet coupling of your living love and in the living friendship of your fiery
divinity, you lead with you in the most blessed circular dance in
heaven[79] thousands upon thousands of the very brightest virgins.
385   They are adorned, at one with you, in snow-white robes, jubilantly
singing the dulcet songs of everlasting marriage. Ah! O Love, in this
misery so guard me under the shadow of your charity that after this
exile when, spotless, I enter beneath your guidance into your sanctuary among the band of virgins, one small vein of your divine
390   friendship may refresh me, and one mellifluous fruition alone may
satiate me. Let all things say Amen, Amen.

---

76. This is part of Gertrud's biblically influenced vocabulary in which terms such as *adeps*,
pinguis and their derivatives are used favorably in the meaning of abundance, riches, happiness,
delight. See also Bernard, SC 7.6, 12.1 or 12.4.

77. Cf. Ho 14:6. This image (see also VI, 692) is quite common in mystical literature. Cf.
Lüers, 270f.

78. 1 Co 12:31.

79. The metaphor of the mystical dance, i.e. the dance in heaven (cf. also VI, 663), is often
found in Mechthild of Magdeburg and other mystics, describing the state of the soul in union
with the divine. It goes back to patristic literature. Cf. Lüers, 267f.

IV

FOLLOWING CHRIST[1]

YOU WILL SPIRITUALLY CELEBRATE your profession or vow with a renewal of new fervor, through these fieriest desires and prayers, dedicating all of yourself as a holocaust[2] and an offering to God, in pleasing scent.

I entreat your exceedingly great mercy, Father almighty, merciful,   5
clement, lovingly-kind, gracious, and so unwavering above malice.[3]
Dry twig [that I am], I have, alas, alas, paid no attention to the season for my pruning[4] there where you planted me in this most holy religion, but have spent all the time of my life in much barrenness.   10
With your merciful and charitable sight deign to look upon me through your innate goodness, through the love of your very cherished mother, our most glorious patron saint, the Virgin Mary, and through the intercession of the most blessed Benedict, our venerable lawmaker. Then, growing altogether strong in you, I may again   15
become green and, sanctified in truth,[5] again begin to flower.[6] I may become a true worshipper of holy religion and a true observer of the spiritual life, and may bear the fruit of total virtue and holiness for

---

1. 'Exercise of the Soul's Profession to God'.

2. Although 'holocaust' has taken on a specific meaning to describe the suffering and death of millions of Jews in the concentration camps during World War II, we have retained the biblical use here.

3. Jl 2:13.

4. Sg 2:12.

5. Jn 17:17.

6. Gertrud may have in mind the Middle High German expression *grüenen und bluien* (to green and to flower). Separate and as a pair, these terms are often used in the texts of the thirteenth and fourteenth century German mystics. As Lüers explains (136–138), the terms denote the soul's participation in the rejuvenating power of the Trinity.

you, my lover, that at the time of vintage, that is, on the day of my
20   death, I may be found in your presence in all perfection of religion,
fully mature, and consummated. Amen.

For the blessing, [say]:
May your divine almightiness, wisdom and goodness, my God,
25   my dulcet love, bless me; and may it make me come after you with
a readiest will, truly deny myself and, with a most resolute heart,
spirit, and soul follow you in a most perfect way. Amen.

At this point, invoke the grace of the Holy Spirit:
O my gentleness and cherishing-love, my God, my mercy. Ah!
30   Send your Holy Spirit straightway from above and create in me a
new heart and a new spirit.[7] Let your anointing teach me all things[8]
because I have chosen you out of thousands,[9] and I cherish you
more dearly above all love and above the love of my soul. May the
virtue of my soul grow fat in that comeliness and beauty of charity
35   that you yearn for, because I desire you passionately. Ah! Make me
appear in your presence becomingly. Amen.

Antiphon: Come![10]
And behold, I come to you whom I have loved, in whom I have
believed, whom I have cherished.

40   *Prayer*: You, the exhilaration of my spirit, you, the praise of my
heart and mouth, my Jesus: I will follow you wherever you go.[11]
Now that you have claimed my heart and possessed it as your own,
for eternity you cannot be taken away from me.

Antiphon: Come!
45   And behold, I come to you whom I have loved, in whom I have
believed, whom I have cherished.

---

7. Ezk 18:31.
8. 1 Jn 2:27.
9. Sg 5:10
10. Cf. III, 106f.
11. Lk 9:57.

Prayer: My cherished one, I hold you tight to my heart, my Jesus, in an inseparable embrace of charity. Behold, having seized you, I now hold you with the love of all my heart: even if you bless me a thousand times I will never more let you go.[12]

Antiphon: Come, daughters! 50
And behold, I come to you whom I have loved, in whom I have believed, whom I have cherished.

Prayer: May all the efficacy and virtue of your divinity praise you for me; may all the friendship and affection of your humanity give satisfaction to you for me; may all the magnificence and imperial majesty of your Trinity glorify, magnify, and honor you yourself, in 55 yourself for me, with that highest praise through which you alone are sufficient to yourself and through which, making amends in yourself for the defects of all creation, you bring [everything] to perfection in yourself. Amen.

Antiphon: Hear me, I will teach you the fear of the Lord![13]

Prayer: Ah Jesus, good shepherd,[14] make me hear and 60 acknowledge your voice apart from everything that keeps me from you. Lift me up in your arms. Make me, your sheep newly delivered in your Spirit, rest against your breast.[15] There teach me how I may fear you.[16] There show me how I may cherish you. There, instruct me how I may follow you. Amen. 65

Antiphon: Come to him and be enlightened: and your faces shall not be confounded.[17]

---

12. Gn 32:26 (28).
13. See *Pontificale*, 127f.
14. Jn 10:11.
315. Cf. Is 40:11.
16. Fear and love are understood as being in harmony with and dependent on each other. This passage calls to mind William of Saint Thierry, *On Contemplating God*, II. 58: '. . . to love and fear God is nothing other than to be of one spirit with him. For to fear God and keep his commandments, that is the whole man.'
17. Ps 33:6 (34:5).

Prayer: Behold, I am approaching you, O consuming fire, my God. Ah! Devouring me, a speck of dust, in the fiery vigor of your
70   love, consume me utterly and absorbe me into yourself. Behold, I am approaching you, O my dulcet light. Ah! Let your face light up over me¹⁸ so that my darkness may become like noonday in your presence. Behold, I am approaching you, O most blessed union. Ah! Make me one with you by the glue of living love.

75   *Psalm*: To the Lord belongs the earth.¹⁹

Antiphon: This is the generation of those who seek the Lord, who seek the face of the God of Jacob.²⁰

Prayer: Make me, dulcet Jesus, to be listed and numbered in the generation of those who know you, God of Israel; among the
80   generation of those who seek your face, God of Jacob; in the generation of those who cherish you, God of hosts. Ah! That I, an innocent woman, with [clean] hands and a clean heart, may accept your blessing and mercy, God, my savior.

Psalm: Have mercy on me, O God.²¹

85   *Antiphon*: Create a clean heart in me, God; renew the upright spirit within my viscera.²²

Prayer: In the abyss²³ of your charity thoroughly immerse me, who have been cast down. Ah! O love, give gratuitously, cleansing me from every spot in the laver of your grace; renew me in you, O my true life.

90   *Psalm*: He who lives in the aid [of the most high].²⁴

---

18. Ps 118 (119):135.
19. Ps 23(24).
20. Ps 23(24):6. An antiphon found in a thirteenth century antiphonal. (Hart, 180.)
21. Ps 50(51):1.
22. Ps 50(51):12.
23. The word *abyssum* is frequently used by Gertrud, both denoting an 'abyss of misery' (as in III, 97) and 'the abyss of God's mercy' (III, 193) or God's love. As a traditional term in mysticism, its usage may go back to Ps 41:8 (42–43:7), as Lüers suggests (119).
24. Ps 90(91).

Antiphon: He who lives in the aid of the most high will remain under the protection of the God of heaven.[25]

Prayer: Keeper of my soul and my refuge on the day of evil, in every temptation shade me with your shoulders of defense; enclose 95 me with the shield of truth.[26] May you yourself be with me in all my tribulation. [You who are] my hope, from every danger to body and soul always defend and protect me. Ah! And after this exile, show me yourself, my dulcet salvation. Amen.

Litany: 100
Lord have mercy. Christ have mercy. Lord have mercy.

Holy Trinity, one God: grant that my heart may fear you, cherish you, follow you because you are my true love.

Holy Mary, paradise of holiness, lily of purity, be the guide and guardian of my chastity, for in you is all the grace of life and truth. 105

All holy angels and archangels, obtain for me service agreeable to this king [that I may offer] with body and soul. To serve him is to reign—him whom you stand by, ministering to without any weariness, with ineffable jubilation. 110

Saint John the Baptist, obtain for me enlightenment through that true light to whom you came to bear witness.[27]

O my Father Abraham, obtain for me that faith and obedience which led you to friendship with the living God.

O Moses, dear to God, obtain for me that spirit of mildness, 115 peace, and charity which made you worthy to hold discourse face to face with the Lord of majesty.[28]

O David, venerable king and prophet, obtain for me the wholeness of fidelity, promptitude, and humility that made you a man after God's own heart,[29] to be truly pleasing and dear to God 120 the king.

---

25. Ps 90(91):1.
26. Cf. Ps 90(91):4–5.
27. Jn 1:7.
28. Ex 33:11.
29. Ac 13:22.

All holy patriarchs and prophets, obtain for me a spirit of comprehension and of understanding.

125   Saint Peter, first of the apostles, by your authority deliver me from the bonds of all my sins.

Saint Paul, chosen vessel,[30] obtain for me the gift of true cherishing-love.

O my dear John, disciple whom Jesus cherished,[31] obtain for me that loving-kindness, spotlessness, and holiness of spirit which the
130   flower (and Son of that lily whose tender guardian you were) yearns for in me.

All holy apostles, brothers and friends of Jesus Christ, my spouse, obtain for me union with him in an inseparable charity.

Saint Stephen, chosen as the protomartyr, obtain for me that
135   thirst to be martyred for the love of Christ so that he himself may become my help who consoled you in death.

Saint Lawrence, unconquered soldier, obtain for me the love stronger than death with which you triumphed over the conflagration and the torturer.

Saint George, flower of martyrs, obtain for me an unconquered
140   spirit in the service of God.

All holy martyrs, obtain for me dulcet patience so that I am prepared, for the love of Jesus, to expose body and soul.

Saint Gregory, apostolic shepherd, obtain for me vigilant perseverance in the resolve of my holy religion until the very end of my
145   life.

Saint Augustine, mirror of the church, obtain for me a life [lived] altogether for God and the church.

O very noble foundation of all of monastic life[32], my father Benedict, cherished by God, obtain for me such steadfastness of the ra-
150   tional soul in the hardship of spiritual life that with you I may receive the prize of eternal life.

All holy confessors, obtain for me the clothing of the confession

---

30. Ac 9:15.
31. Jn 13:23.
32. *Religio* is here used in the restricted sense of the 'monastic state of life'.

[of faith] and beauty[33] so that all my life and actions may confess the Lord's compassion in all his work.

Saint Catherine, wounded by divine charity, obtain for me a dis- 155 dain for everything earthly and yearning for Jesus alone.

Saint Agnes, tender follower of the Lamb, obtain for me fiery charity to cherish my spouse Jesus—you who find glory in being bound in love [and] pledged in faith, and who have gone into his in- ner chamber. 160

Saint Mary Magdalene, most fervent lover of Jesus Christ, obtain for me the most diligent observance of holy religion.

All holy virgins and widows, obtain for me progress in all holiness of spiritual life so that I may be able to come to the fruit a hundred- 165 fold.[34]

All saints and chosen ones of God, obtain for me such observance of holy religion that thereby I may come with you to that homeland of eternal life which knows nothing but joys, where God is all in all.[35] 170

Be favorable toward my sins and thoughtlessness, Lord, and deign to make amends for all errors of my wasted way of life by your most perfect way of life.

From all faintheartedness and tempestuousness of spirit, from all perversity and carnality of heart, from all blindness and sterility of 175 mind, from all thoughtlessness and depravity of conduct, free me, Lord.

By all the viscera of your fatherly mercy,[36] give me understanding and instruct me in the resolve of this religion, which I now profess in your presence, because I confess that I am nothing and without 180 you neither know anything nor am capable of anything.

Through her who gave you birth, lead me onto the spotless nar- row path so that I may become pleasing to you in body and soul.

I, your unworthy and prodigal daughter (who have, alas, through my exigent sins lost the name daughter) trusting in your fatherly 185 loving-kindness, beg you, look upon me according to the multitude

---

33. Ps 95(96):6.
34. Lk 8:8.
35. 1 Co 15:28.
36. Lk 1:78.

of your mercies,[37] and, abolishing all my failure in loving-kindness, heed me.

190   That in holy religion you deign to bestow upon me a spirit unconquered, a heart sensitive, a rational soul ready, and a body suitable:[38] we beg you to hear us.

That you deign to instill grace, and the savor and love of spiritual life into me: we beg you to hear us.

195   That you make me renounce this age perfectly and cling to you with total devotion: we beg you to hear us.

That you make me faithful in my performance of this holy religion and grant me perseverance in this resolve: we beg you to hear us.

200   That upon all of us who serve you in this place, you deign to bestow unity of spirit in the bond of charity and peace;[39] and, after this life, deign to lead us through to the promised reward of your glory: we beg you to hear us.

That by all your divine authority, you deign to absolve me from all my sins and to embolden me in my holy resolve; and, by all your human affection, [deign] to show yourself placable to me, and in all

205   this fully heed me: we beg you to hear us.

Jesus, Son of the living God, to you alone is known all that causes my desire; fashion me after your own heart: we beg you to hear us.

210   Lamb of God, on this way where I walk, hold my right hand lest I grow faint.

Lamb of God, make me faithfully fulfill with your co-operation what I have begun in your name.

Lamb of God, do not let my sins hinder me but let your compas-

215   sion move me forward in all these things.

Christ hear me; at the hour of death gladden me in your salvation.

Lord have mercy. Christ have mercy. Lord have mercy.

---

37. Ps 68:17(69:16).
38. St Gertrud's enumeration here of *spiritus* (spirit), *cor* (heart), *animus* (rational soul) and *corpus* (body) suggests a comparison with William of Saint Thierry's *Golden Epistle*, 25–27, xii, 41–45. Cf. also ExspSCh, 138, n. 2.
39. Eph 4:3.

Prayer: God, who with the utmost art plant and guard all virtue, make me, who am like some small grain unworthy of your true 220 seed, grow strong in the resolve of holy religion and increase a thousandfold the fruit of a more perfect life and to the very end of my life persevere, faithful and unwearied, in your holy service.

With this responsory invoke divine wisdom to help you: 225

Responsory: Lord, send forth wisdom from the throne of your magnitude that she may be with me and labor with me that I may know what is acceptable in your presence at all times.

Verse: Lord, grant me Wisdom that sits by your throne so that I 230 may know what is acceptable in your presence at all times.[40]

At this point, you will give the hand-written document of your profession[41] to the Lord, saying:[42]

[Middle High German]	[Latin]
My beloved Jesus Christ, I desire to enter with you into a beloved rule so that I may renew and remake my life in you. Ah! Place my life in the guardianship of your Holy Spirit so that I may keep your commandments at all times. In dear joy make my conduct suitable to you in dear peace. Flood my senses with the light of your love so that you alone may teach and guide me, and convert me within. Sink my spirit	My most cherished Jesus, I wish to take up the rule of love with you whereby I may be capable of renewing my life and spending it in you. Ah! Place my life in the guardianship of your Holy Spirit so that I may be found most ready for your commandments at all times. Make my conduct like yours: make me firm in your love and in peace. Enclose my senses in the light of your charity so that you alone may teach, guide,

235

---

40. This Responsory and Verse are based on Ws 9:4 and 9:10.

41. According to RB 58.19-20, the novice, at the time of profession, 'states his promise in a document, . . .writes out this document himself, . . .and with his own hands lays it on the altar.'

42. Lines 234-245 constitute part of the Middle High German text in Lanspergius' edition. Again, the column at the left translates the Middle High German, the column on the right renders Lanspergius' Latin version into English.

240 so firmly into your Spirit—
quickly down into its ground—
that I may be truly buried in
you. And let me be so fully
transported out of myself into
union with you that nobody
may know of my grave in you
except your living love alone,
which may place its seal on it.
Amen.

245

and instruct me within the penetralia of my heart. Absorb my
spirit in your Spirit so powerfully and so deeply that, truly, I
may be totally buried in you
and grow faint in myself in
union with you; and that no
one else, apart from your love,
may know of my burial in you.
There, may love lock me under
its seal and entrust me to you in
an indivisible nexus. Amen.

At this point, turn back to the Lord, examining what the prime
obedience may be that his love enjoins on you.

My cherished one cries out to me: Put me as a seal on your heart
250 [and] on your arm: for cherishing-love is strong as death.[43]

With this responsory, prepare yourself in total readiness to enter
the way of beautiful cherishing-love with the Lord.

Responsory:[44] Let me cherish you, Lord, my virtue: Lord, my
stronghold and refuge, and my liberator.

255 *Verse:* Praising, I invoke the Lord and will be saved from my enemies, Lord, my stronghold, my refuge, and my liberator.[45]

In accepting the yoke of the holy rule, [say]:

Receive me, holy Father, in your most clement fatherliness so
260 that on the race track of this holy resolve where I have begun to run
for the sake of your love, I may accept you yourself as [my] prize[46]
and eternal inheritance.

---

43. Sg 8:6.
44. The Latin masculine endings in this particular passage come about through direct quota-
tions from Ps 17(18).
45. Ps 17:3–4(18:2–3)—This verse appears in a thirteenth century antiphonal. Hart, 181.
46. 1 Co 9:24.

Receive me, most loving Jesus, into your most gracious brotherli-
ness: may you bear with me the burden of the day's heat;[47] and may 265
I have you as consolation for all my labor, as my partner on the
road, as guide and companion.

Receive me, Holy Spirit, God love, in your most lovingly-kind
mercy and charity: may I have you as master and teacher of my entire life and as the most dulcet lover of my heart. Amen. 270

At this point, throw yourself down in the presence of the Lord:
Lord have mercy. Christ have mercy. Lord have mercy.

Psalm: Have mercy on me, O God.[48]

Say: I come to your feet, most loving Father. Behold, my sins
have made a separation between you and me. Ah! Have mercy on 275
me according to the multitude of your mercy,[49] break the wall of
my old way of life which keeps me from you;[50] and drag me so
vehemently toward you that I may, in the gentleness of your inextinguishable cherishing-love, wisely follow you by loving.

Prayer: Ah lovingly-kind Jesus, although the will [to do what is 280
good] is in me, I do not find [the strength] to accomplish it.[51] Therefore, by the co-operation of your grace and through the spotless law
of your love, turn my soul from the frailty of the human condition
toward you in such a way that I may untiringly run the way of your
commandments[52] and cling inseparably to you. Be with me, my
Lord, aiding me always and making me strong in the work that I 285
have taken up for the love of your love.[53]

---

47. Mt 20:12.

48. Ps 50(51).

49. Dn 3:42.

50. Cf. Is 5:5. This passage is considered a reference to *Legatus* II (139).16 where Gertrud
relates her mystical experience.

51. Rm 7:18.

52. Ps 118(119):32. Running the way of the commandments, cf. RB (Prol.49).

53. This phrase, 'for the love of your love' (also in V, 35 and *Legatus* III, 41. 1, 8 and
elsewhere), is a direct quotation from William of Saint Thierry's *On Contemplating God*, 37.2.
(ExspSCh, 144, n.4).

For putting on the holy habit, say this prayer:

O come, noble love, by which I, an ignoble reed, under your flower-like aspect, may be like a lily[54] planted by the right hand of
290   your most outstanding divinity in the deepest valley of holy humility, beside the water of your overflowing charity, beside the water of your great indulgence and loving-kindness. There I, dry stalk of your planting, who am within myself totally nothing and empty, may again become fully green through the fatness of your spirit and
295   again flourish in you, O my most dulcet morning. Thus, in you, let me strip off my old self and its acts to be able to be clothed with a new self[55] that has been created according to God, in justice and holiness of truth.[56]

Responsory:[57] For the love of my Lord Jesus Christ I have contemned the kingdom of this world and all the adornments of this age. It is he whom I have seen, whom I have loved, in whom I have believed, whom I have cherished.
300   What more is there now for me in this world,[58] O my dear Jesus? Behold, not even in heaven is there anything apart from you that I have wanted:[59] you alone I love, you I desire, you I cherish, you I yearn for, you I thirst for, you I love. In you, I grow wholly faint, my cherished, my cherished one. Ah! Transport me over into the flame of your living conflagration and make me now cling to you so
305   totally that, having left my body behind at the hour of death, I may for eternity be well in you. For my soul loves you, my heart desires you, my virtue cherishes you, and all my life passing from me has already gone after you. O Jesus, dearest of all dear ones, to you my
310   heart says, 'You are my dearest dear one, all my true and secure joy, my best share, whom alone my soul loves and cherishes'.

---

54. Cf. Sg 2:1.
55. Col 3:9–10.
56. Eph 4:24.
57. The Latin text simply gives the first few words of this responsory and then states: *ut supra* 'as above' referring back to the previous quotation of this text (III, 303ff.). We have filled in the text for the reader's convenience here and in all other similar cases.
58. This paragraph again appears to be influenced by William of Saint Thierry's *On Contemplating God*, 42–47.5–6. Cf. also ExspSCh, 146, n. 3.
59. Cf. Ps 72(73):25.

Approaching communion, throw[60] yourself entirely into God to
live for him alone:

What am I, my God, life of my soul? Alas, alas, how far from
you! Behold, I am, as it were, a speck of dust that the wind flings   315
from the face of the earth.[61] Ah! ah! By virtue of your charity deign
to drive so powerfully the hot wind[62] of your almighty love and, in
the hurricane of your spirit, to fling me into you with such impetu-
osity and to rescue me [in such a way] in the bosom of your lovingly-
kind care that I truly begin to grow faint and be in ecstasy[63] in you,
O my dulcet love. There, there, grant that I may lose myself in you,   320
to leave myself so wholly behind in you that no vestige of me remains in me, just as a grain of dust having been tossed about leaves
no trace there of its tossing about. Ah! ah! Transport me so thoroughly into the affection of your love that all my imperfection may be   325
annihilated in you and that, outside of you, I may have no spirit any
longer. Ah! Grant that I so squander myself in you that for eternity
I will find myself nowhere but in you. Amen.

At this point, desire to be consummated in the Lord: 330

What am I, my God, love of my heart? Alas, alas, how unlike you
I am! Behold, it is as if I were a tiny droplet of your goodness, and
you the full ocean of total gentleness. Ah! O love, love, open, open
on me, the very little one, the viscera of your loving-kindness. Pour
on me all the cataracts of your most gracious fatherliness. Break   335
over me all the fountains of the great abyss[64] of your unlimited mercy. Let the depth of your charity absorb me. Let me be submerged
into the abyss of the ocean of your most indulgent loving-kindness.
Let me perish in the deluge of your living love just as a drop perishes

---

60. The verb used here is literally 'fling', which is the same word also used twice in the
following paragraph.

61. Ps 1:4.

62. Cf. Is 21:1.

63. Only twice in the *Exercitia spiritualis* is *excessus mentis* mentioned. In this case it appears in
the context of being lost in or made ecstatic with love; in V, 30 ecstasy is gained by 'seeing
God'.

64. Gn 7:11.

340   in the depth of the ocean's fullness. Let me die, let me die in the tor-
      rent[65] of your immense compassion, just as the little spark of fire
      dies in the stream's strongest current. Let the raindrops of your
      cherishing-love envelop me. Let the cup of your love carry my life
      away. Let the secret counsel of your wisest love bring about and
345   perfect glorious death in me through life-sustaining love.[66] There,
      there, I will lose my life in you where you live eternally, O my love,
      God of my life. Amen.

      At this point, desire to be buried in the living God:
      What am I, my God, my holy gentleness? Alas, alas, I have be-
350   come the scum of all your creatures.[67] But you are my great trust,
      for in you is laid up an abundance for me with which to make
      amends for my thorough wastefulness. Ah! O love, love, love, amass
      now over me a heap of your immense goodness and indulgence.
      Crush me with the weight of your loving-kindness and unlimited
355   clemency. Make me expire in the dulcet expiration of your Spirit
      and fall asleep beneath the covering of your love.[68] In tasting your
      pleasantness, I am alive; let me surrender my spirit in order that,
      passing over from myself to you, O my dulcet loveliness, I may walk
      pleasantly, may fall into your embraces, and may truly be buried in
360   the kiss of your mellifluous love.
      Envelop me in the linen of your dear redemption. Em-balm me
      with the spices of your precious death. Lay me in the marble tomb
      of your heart which was pierced by a lance, hiding me under the
      stone of the most dulcet regard of your mellifluous face so that you
365   may take care of me for eternity. There, there, my cherished one,
      let me be buried in the very dulcet shadow of your fatherly cherish-
      ing-love. Let me rest. Let me rest. Let me rest in the sempiternal
      memory of your precious and living friendship. Ah ah! In you, O

---

65. The noun *profluvium* literally reads 'flow', but the translation seems too weak in the context of this forceful metaphor.

66. This phrase almost amounts to a definition of 'Minnetod' or *mors mystica*—a key term
for medieval mysticism. Cf. also Haas, 'Mors mystica', 304–392 [passim].

67. 1 Co 4:13. Cf. also Bernard, SC 25.5.

68. Cf. Ps 62:8 (63:7).

strong love, let my flesh dry up. In you, O life-sustaining love, let my life expire. In you, O dulcet love, let my entire substance be reduced to ashes. And in the mellifluous light of your countenance, let my soul rest for eternity. Amen.   370

Then, giving thanks, recite the canticle, My soul magnifies the Lord,[69] together with this prayer:

To you, God of my life, life-giver of my soul, to you, my most dulcet lover, Father, spouse, and my provider, I present the entire   375
treasure of my love in the brazier of your burning Spirit, in the white-hot furnace of your living love. Because of you, because of you, O dearest of all dear ones, I enter on rough ways at this hour knowing that your mercy is better than life itself.[70]   380

Ah! O my cherished one, by your divine virtue, gird me (who presume upon your loving-kindness) for war with the armor of your Spirit in order to put behind me all the crafty devices of my enemies.[71] Through your inextinguishable charity, cast beneath me   385
everything in me that does not altogether live for you alone. May I, then, cherish you with the dulcet assistance of your living cherishing-love, drawn to and refreshed by the life-giving pleasantness of your love. May I cherish you, O my dulcet virtue, while cheerfully carrying under your guidance the pleasant yoke and the light burden[72] of your love. Then all the labor of my serving you, my cherished one, may be seen [to last] a few days because of the great-   390
ness of your love.

May the dulcet temperateness of your Spirit abbreviate and alleviate for me all the burden of the day's heat.[73] And deign to intertwine all the operation and exercise of my life with the co-operation of the vital cherishing-love of your life. Then let my soul magnify you for eternity; let all my life serve you untiringly and my spirit   395

---

69. Lk 1:46–55, the daily Vespers canticle.
70. Ps 62:4 (63:3).
71. Cf. Ps 17:41 (18:40).
72. Mt 11:30.
73. Mt 20:12.

exult in you, God, my savior;[74] and let all my thought and action
consist of praise and thanksgiving for you. Amen.

Having finished all this, commend yourself to the Lord with the
canticle, Now you release your servant, O Lord, according to your
word, in peace.[75]

400   Ah! Now, O love, my king and my God, now, O my Jesus, my
dear, receive me in the most gracious care of your divine heart.
There, there, so that I may live entirely for you, glue me to your
love.

Ah! Now release me into the great ocean of your mercy's abyss:
405   There, there, commit me to the viscera of your overflowing loving-kindness. Ah! Now cast me into the voracious flame of your living love. There, there, transmit me into you until my soul and spirit
are reduced to ashes in the conflagration. Ah! And at the hour of
my passing away, commit me to the providence of your fatherly
charity.

410   There, there, my dulcet salvation, console me with the sight of
your mellifluous presence. There, by the taste of your dear ransom,
with which you have redeemed me, recreate me. There, with the
loving voice of your beautiful cherishing-love, call me to you.
There, in the embrace of your most indulgent placability receive
me.[76] There, into the dulcet expiration of your pleasant-flowing
415   Spirit draw me [to you] and draw me in, and imbibe me. There, in
the kiss of perfect union of your fruition immerse me forever. And
grant me then to see you, to have you, to enjoy you eternally in the
greatest happiness, for my soul has yearned for you, O Jesus, dearest
of all dear ones. Amen.

---

74. Lk 1:46f.
75. Lk 2:29.
76. This passage combines all the spiritual senses except for smell.

V

MYSTICAL UNION[1]

A S OFTEN AS YOU WANT to be at leisure for love, withdraw your heart from all inordinate affection, hindrances, and phantasms, choosing the day and an opportune time for this purpose—at least three hours on that day, that is, in the morning, at noon, and in the evening—making amends for never having cherished your Lord God with all your heart, all your soul and with all your virtue.[2] And now, with all [your] affection, all devotion and intention, may you join yourself to God in prayer, as if you saw the spouse Jesus himself present, who assuredly is present in your soul.

And early in the morning, as if running to meet your God, say this prayer with these three verses:

God, my God; for you I watch at daybreak. For you my soul has thirsted,

for you my flesh, how many ways! In a desert land, and where there is no way and no water:

so in the sanctuary, have I come before you to see your virtue and your glory.[3]

Ah! O God, love, you alone are my entire and true love. You are my dearest salvation, all my hope and joy[4] and my supreme and best

---

1. 'Exercise of Divine Love'.
2. Mt 22:37.
3. Ps 62:2–3 (63:1–2).
4. *Amor* (love), *spes* (hope) and *gaudium* (joy) belong to the 'affections of the soul'. See Doyère, 'Affectiones animae', *Legatus* III (143), 352–356.

73

20   good. My God, my dearest love, in the morning I will stand before
       you and will see⁵ that you yourself are everlasting pleasantness and
       gentleness. You are what my heart thirsts for. You are the entire
       sufficiency of my spirit. The more I taste you, the more I hunger
       [for you]; the more I drink, the more I thirst.

       O God, love, the vision of you is for me like the very brightest
       day: that one day which, in the courts of the Lord, is better above
25   thousands;⁶ for this alone sighs my soul, that you have redeemed for
       yourself. Ah! When will you satisfy me with the gentleness of your
       mellifluous face? How my soul yearns and pines for the fat of your
       pleasantness.⁷ Behold, I have chosen and chosen above all to be a
       castaway in the house of my God so that I may be able to aspire to
       the refreshment of your most dulcet face.

30   O love, to see you is to be in ecstasy in God. To cling to you is to
       be joined to God by a nuptial contract. O serenest light of my soul,
       very brightest morning, ah, break into day in me now and begin so
       to shine for me that by your light I may see light⁸ and that through
       you my night may be turned into day. By the love of your love, O
35   my dearest morning, let me reckon everything that you are *not* as if
       it were nothing and void.⁹ Ah! Visit me now in the morning at
       daybreak that I may suddenly be transformed entirely into you.

       O love, not light-bearing but God-bearing,¹⁰ come to me now
       bountifully that I may dulcetly melt in you. Brought to nothing in
40   myself, let me flow into you completely so that from now on I may
       never be capable of collecting myself again, [even] temporarily, but
       may stay glued to you eternally.

       O love, you are that singular exemplar, that foremost comeliness,
       which sees in this age only beneath the wings of seraphs.¹¹ Oh when
45   will such beauty refresh me? O imperial morning star,¹² fulgent with
       divine brightness. Oh when will your presence enlighten me?

---

5. Ps 5:5 (3).
6. Ps 83:11 (84:10).
7. Ps 83:3 (84:2).
8. Ps 35:10 (36:9).
9. Is 40:17.
10. The Latin is *lucifer* and *deifer*.
11. The Biblical allusion is for Is 6:2 where seraphs with six wings by God's throne cover his face.
12. Rv 22:16.

O most lovable radiance, when will you satisfy me with yourself?
If only I might here perceive the fine rays of your Venus-like beauty
for a little while and at least be permitted to anticipate your
gentleness for a short time and pleasantly beforehand to taste you,   50
my best share. Ah! Turn around now a little so that I may fix my
look on you, flower of flowers.

You are the very bright mirror of the holy Trinity, which *there*
one is permitted to look at face to face through the eye of a clean   55
heart, but *here* only obscurely.[13] Ah! Sprinkle me with your purity
and I will be cleansed. Touch my innermost heart with your cleanliness and I will become whiter than snow.[14] Let the greatness of your
charity prevail, I beseech you, and let the copious holiness of your
merits envelop me, lest my unlikeness to Venus keep me from you.   60

Look upon me and see and make me acknowledge and know you.
You cherished me first.[15] You chose me when I had not chosen
you.[16] You run up spontaneously to everyone who thirsts for you:
the whiteness of the eternal light[17] glistens on your fore-   65
head.

Ah! Show me your face[18] and make me contemplate[19] your radiance. Lo, your face, which the most beautiful dawn of divinity il-
luminates, is pleasant and comely.[20] Miraculously your cheeks blush
with *omega* and *alpha*.[21] Very bright eternity burns inextinguishably   70
in your eyes. There God's salvation glows as red for me as a lamp.
There radiant charity sports merrily with luminous truth. The scent
of life breathes forth from you to me. Honey and milk drip down
from your mouth to me.[22]

---

13. 1 Co 13:12.
14. Cf. Ps 50:9 (51:7).
15. 1 Jn 4:19.
16. Cf. Jn 15:16.
17. Ws 7:26.
18. Ps 79:4 (80:3).
19. The sense in which *contemplari* and *contemplatio* (a frequent term in chapters V and VI) are
understood by the mystics is based on 2 Co 4:18: 'And so we have no eyes for things that are visible, but only for things that are invisible'. Cf. *Vocabulaire monastique*, 85–87. Moreover, the term
evokes the monastic life as such, which was during the Middle Ages, as Leclercq states, considered
the contemplative life par excellence. Ibid., 140.
20. Sg 6:3 (4).
21. Rv 1:8. Gertrud reverses the Biblical 'the Alpha and the Omega'.
22. Sg 4:11.

How beautiful you are, O God, Charity,[23] and how lovely, how wondrous and how remarkable in delights, dearest one. Filled with the riches of the imperial Trinity, you, the queen, are seated first on the divine throne. You, wife and spouse of the supreme God, rejoice in always dwelling with him, joined inseparably in cherishing the Son of God.

O love, at the sunset of my life, deign to rise for me early in the morning; and when you see me leave this place of sojourn, make me draw eternal life in you. And grant me so to end this exile that, with you, I may be able to go, without hindrance, to the nuptials of the Lamb[24] and, under your guidance, to discover the true spouse and friend, and be coupled to him in your arms so dearly that, for eternity, I will nevermore be capable of being separated from his grasp.

O love, O key of David,[25] unlock and open to me, then, the holy of holies, that, sent in by you, I may gladly, without delay, see the God of gods in Sion,[26] whose mellifluous countenance my soul desires and yearns for.

At noonday, approach the spouse blazing in love for you so that he, the sun of justice, may kindle your luke-warmness[27] with the fervor of his cherishing-love, that the coal of divine love may burn inextinguishably on the altar of your heart. And say this prayer with these verses:

Let me cherish you, my Lord, my strength; my God, my helper; my protector and the horn of my salvation.[28]

Prayer: Ah! O love, first-blossoming flower of my love—you, my dearest betrothal gift and my nuptial dowry. Behold! For your sake

---

23. The following paragraphs speak of the feminine aspect of the divinity, i.e. *caritas* (charity).

24. Rv 19:7.

25. Rv 3:7.

26. Ps 83:8 (84:7).

27. Gertrud's own inner conversion (*Legatus* II.23) was that from tepidity to fervor. The term *tepidus/tepiditas*, therefore, plays a special role and reoccurs in VII, 61, 434 and 659. The phrase *nos tepidi* (lukewarm as we are) is also in RB 18:25. Cf. also S. Couneson, 'Quelques côtés humains du caractère de Sainte Gertrude', *Revue liturgique et monastique* 22 (1936/37) 409–418. As Doyère comments: 'La médiocrité et la nonchalance lui (i.e. Gertrud) font horreur'. *Legatus* I, II (139), 19.

28. Ps 17:2–3 (18:1–2).

I have despised this age and I have reckoned all worldly joy like mud
on my feet that I might be able to aspire to marriage with you.   100
Ah! Admit me to the secret of your charity. Lo! My heart already
burns for the kiss of your love.²⁹ Open for me the private bedchamber of your beautiful cherishing-love. Lo! My soul thirsts for
the embrace of intimate union with you.

Ah! Prepare now the banquet of your plentiful mercy, inviting   105
me to the table of your gentleness. Set before me the very dulcet
meal of your sempiternal favor, which alone can embolden my
spirit.

Ah! Let us now feast together, O my dearest and supreme good.
You abound and superabound in yourself inestimably in all good-   110
ness, and you impart yourself miraculously to your creation.

Ah! Refresh me bountifully with yourself. For how will a spark
live if not in its fire? Or how can a drop [of water] exist if not in its
fountain?   115

Ah! Let your dear fieriness now devour and envelop me totally,
spirit and soul together, just as your almighty liberality has power
over a speck of dust. O love, O most dulcet noonday heat, your
holy idleness in full peace delights me above all things. Your sab-   120
baths of homage are stilled by the presence of God; yet for the most
serene face of the spouse they overflow with grace.

Ah! O my cherished one, chosen and chosen above all, over all
creation! Now in yourself, make clear to me, and show me where
you pasture, where you lie asleep at noonday.³⁰ Lo! My spirit
seethes and burns for the gentleness of your day of rest.   125

O love, here, under the mellifluous shadow of your charity, all
my hope and trust repose. Israel dwells trustfully in the bosom of
your peace.³¹ My soul passionately yearns for the solemnity of this
sabbath of homage.

---

29. Cf. Sg 1:1.

30. Key terms in this entire passage (lines 119–125) connote the state of contemplation, such
as *otium* (idleness), *sabbatum* (sabbath), *pax* (peace), *pascare* (pasture), and *cubere in meridie* (lie
asleep at noonday)—the latter influenced by Sg 1:6(7). For a thorough discussion of *quies,
otium, vacatio, sabbatum* (all used in Gertrud's text), see Jean Leclercq, *Otia monastica. Études sur
le vocabulaire de la contemplation au moyen-âge.* Studia Anselmiana 51 (Rome 1963) 13–59.

31. Jr 23:6.

130   O love, the fruition of you is that worthiest coupling of your
       Word and the soul which is brought about by perfect union with
       God. To use you is to become intertwined in God. To enjoy you is
       to be one with God. You are that peace which surpasses all un-
       derstanding[32] and [you are] the road by which one comes to the in-
       ner chamber.

135   Oh, if only it happened to me, too, miserable as I am, to repose
       for a moment under your dearest cloak of cherishing-love so that
       my heart might be emboldened by one consolatory utterance of
       your living Word, or that my soul might hear this good and pleasant
       word from your mouth: 'I am your salvation;[33] behold, now the
       bedchamber of my heart is open to you.'

140   Why, then, O love so unwavering, have you deeply loved
       someone so foul, so ugly, if not to make her beautiful in you? Your
       lovingly-kind charity attracts and allures me, O tender flower of the
       virgin Mary.

       Let me not be confounded in my expectation[34] but grant me to
145   find rest for my soul in you. I have found nothing more desirable,[35] I
       have judged nothing more lovable, I have wished for nothing more
       dear than to be held tight, O love, in your embraces, to rest under the
       wings of my Jesus, and to dwell in the tabernacle of divine charity.

       O love, O radiant noonday, I would die a thousand times to be at
150   rest in you. If only you would bend to me your face of such beauti-
       ful cherishing-love, O dearest one.

       Oh, if I were granted to come exceedingly close to you so that I
       might now find myself not only next to you but within you. Then,
       through you, sun of justice, flowers of all the virtues might arise in
155   me, [who am] dust and ashes. With you as a husband, my Lord,
       such fecundity might enter my soul that the renowned offspring of
       total perfection would be born in me. Then, having been snatched

32. Ph 4:7.
33. Ps 34 (35):3.
34. Ps 118 (119):116. RB 58:21 quotes this psalm passage in the context of the novice's acceptance into the monastic community. See also the tenth century Pontifical, 41.
35. Syntax and diction suggest the influence of the hymn *Dulcis Jesu memoria*, stanzas 2 and
8. Cf. André Wilmart, 'Le *Jubilus* sur le nom de Jésus dit de Saint Bernard', *Ephemerides
Liturgicae* 57 (1943) 3–283 with the full text of the poem. Cf. ExspSCh, 168, n. 2.

from the valley of this misery, I might be able to glory [in you]
forever in the presence of your desirable face; for you, mirror without spot, have not scorned to be, in truth, coupled with a sinner like   160
me.

Ah! O charity, at the hour of death let your words better than
wine[36] refresh me and let your lips gentler than honey[37] and the
honey comb[38] console me. And may you yourself be the way for
me that I may then not stray along the wrong way, but, aided by
you, O queen, may come without hindrance to the radiance and
fatness of the divine desertland where I may gladly deserve thor-   165
oughly to enjoy the mellifluous presence of my spouse, God and
Lamb. May all things say Amen.

In the evening, entirely melting and growing faint while waiting
to enjoy the sempiternal vision of the mellifluous face of God and
the Lamb, rush into the embrace of the spouse Jesus, your lover;   170
altogether like a busy bee[39] that clings with a kiss to his amorous
heart, plead for a kiss from him—[one] so efficacious that now you
die to yourself, and in your death you cross over into God and
become one spirit with him[40] crying out in thirst:

As the hart desires for the fountain of water   175
so my soul desires for you, God.
My soul has thirsted for the strong living God;
When will I come and appear before the face of God?
My tears have been my bread day and night,
while I am told daily: Where is your God?[41]

Ah! O love, dulcet in [your] kiss, you are that fountain for which   180
I thirst. Behold, my heart seethes for you; if only, if only you, a full

36. Sg 1:1.
37. Cf. Sg 4:11.
38. Ps 18:11 (19:10).
39. This *apis negotiosa* is an example of the wide range of metaphors pertaining to the 'mystical bee' in medieval mysticism. See Louise Gnädinger, 'Rosenwunden' in *Deutsche Barocklyrik*,
eds. Martin Bircher and Alois Maria Haas (Bern/Munich 1973) 97–133.
40. 1 Co 6:17.
41. Ps 41:1–4 (42–43:1–3).

ocean, would absorb me, an ordinary drop, into yourself. You are my soul's living and most dulcet entrance, through which there may be an exit for me from myself into you.

185   Ah! May the saving entrance of your dearest heart be opened to me. Behold, I no longer have my heart with me,[42] but you, O my dearest treasure, preserve it with you in your repository. You are the unique, total, and dearest little substance of my heart. To you alone my little soul has clung fervently.

190   Oh, what a companionship yours is. Truly, truly, being familiar with you is by far better than life. Your scent is like the innermost balsam of divine peace and favor. You are the superabundant and exceedingly rich storehouse of divine consolation. If only, O charity, queen, you led me into your pantry[43] that I might pleasantly
195   taste your better wines, which lie hidden there. Lo, all your vessels are brimful with God and overflowing with the Holy Spirit.

Oh, if what I am yearning for happened to me here and I were granted my dear wish and, in truth, you turned to me and refreshed me with the very pleasant kiss of your favor! If only, O my dearest
200   dear one, I might seize you in my innermost [self] and kiss you warmly so that, truly united with you, I might cling inseparably to you.

O love, you are the very pleasant kiss of the Holy Trinity, which so mightily unites Father and Son. You are that saving kiss which
205   the imperial divinity has pressed upon our humanity through the Son.

O most dulcet kiss, do not let your bonds pass over me, this speck of dust; may your touch as well as your grasp not spare me until I become one spirit with God.[44] Make me truly experience how great
210   are the delights in grasping you, the living God, my most dulcet love, and in being united with you.

O God, love, you are my dearest possession, without which I neither hope nor wish nor yearn for anything else in heaven or on

---

42. The lovers' exchange of hearts is a topos in the secular poetry of the time, the *Minnesang*.
43. Cf. Sg 1:3 (4).
44. 1 Co 6:17.

earth. You are that toward which my purpose and intention extend:
my true inheritance and all my expectation.   215

Ah! O love, may your cherishing-love consummated in me be my
end and consummation. When the evening approaches, show me
the agreement of the nuptial contract that my heart now has
entered into with you. In the countenance of my dearest God, you
[are] the light of the evening star. At the time of my death, deign to   220
appear to me, O my dear and very bright evening, that in you I may
have the wished-for evening of this my sojourn, pleasantly falling
asleep[45] and resting[46] on your breast ([which is] full of all gentleness).

O God, love, let my dissolution become the enveloping of my   225
soul in you that cloaked by you in your royal comeliness, I may appear worthy in the presence of the immortal spouse, in a wedding
dress [and] with a spousal dowry.

Ah! O love, let the hour of my consummation be signed with the
seal[47] of your dear cherishing-love and be stamped with the charac-   230
teristic mark of your eternal favor. Your blessing, distilling plentifully,
may then lead me without hindrance to the threshold of my eternal
reception into you, of sempiternal fruition and possession forever.

O love, O my dearest evening, at the hour of death, let me see   235
you with merriment and gladness. Let that holy flame that continuously burns in you in the fiery vigor of divinity truly purge every
spot from my soul.

O my very gentle evening, when the evening of this life has ar-
rived for me, make me dulcetly lose consciousness in you and ex-   240
perience that most blessed rest which has been prepared in you for
your dear ones. Let the exceedingly calm and agreeable regard of
your beautiful cherishing-love deign to order and arrange my magnificent nuptials. With the riches of your goodness cover and conceal
the poverty and impoverishment of my degenerate life. Let my soul   245
dwell in the delights of your charity with exceeding trust.

---

45. Ps 4:9 (8).

46. This image, partly associated with Ps 4, also refers to the Christ-John-pose at the Last
Supper (Jn 13:23–25) which became a literary topos in medieval spiritual works. From the early
fourteenth century on, the image was also represented in sculpture.

47. Cf. Rv 7:3 and Ezk 9:4.

O love, may you then be for me such an evening that, through
you, my soul may with gladness and exultation bid a dulcet farewell
to my body; and may my spirit, returning to the Lord who gave it,
250   pleasantly rest in peace beneath your shadow. Then, with your own
voice, while most dulcetly playing the cithara, you will say manifest-
ly to me: 'Behold, the bridegroom is coming;[48] now go out to join
yourself more closely to him that he may gladden you by the glory
of his countenance.'

Oh, how happy, how blessed [is the one] whose sojourn ends in
255   you. Alas, for me, alas for me, how long will it be extended?[49] Oh
what a *then* it will be when that very pleasant and lovely *now* arrives;
when the glory of my God, my king, and my spouse is manifested
and appears to me [offering] endless fruition and sempiternal glad-
260   ness; when, in truth, I contemplate and see this desirable, this
wished-for and this lovable face of my Jesus for which my soul has
so long thirsted[50] and whose radiance it has yearned for. Surely then
I will be satisfied and filled by the torrent of his voluptuousness,
which, locked away for so long now, lies hidden for me in the store-
265   house of divinity. Then I will see and contemplate my God, my
dearest love, in whom my spirit and my heart now grow faint.[51]

When, oh when will you show yourself to me so that I may see
and with merriment draw from you, God, the living fountain. Then
I will drink and will become inebriated with the dulcet plentifulness
270   of the living fountain,[52] which distills the delights of the mellifluous
face of him whom my soul desires.[53]

O dulcet face, when will you satisfy me with yourself? Then I will
go into the place of the wonderful tabernacle[54] even to the very
aspect of God; at its threshold my heart is made to groan because I
275   am delayed by my sojourn here. Oh, when will you fill me with

---

48. Mt 25:6.
49. Ps 119:5 (120:6).
50. Ps 41:3 (42–43:2).
51. Ps 72 (73):26.
52. This image (and see V, 434, 483 and VI, 532f.) belongs to the topos of spiritual drunk-
enness. Cf. *Legatus* IV (255), 438f., n. 2, and Lüers, 268–270.
53. Ps 41:2 (42–43:1).
54. Ps 41:5 (42–43:4).

gladness[55] by your mellifluous face? Then I will contemplate and
warmly kiss the true spouse of my soul, my Jesus, to whom it has
already clung in thirst and to whom, at the same time, all my heart
goes out.

Oh, who will free me from the exile of this pilgrimage? Oh, who
will snatch me from the snares of this age? Oh, when will I leave 280
behind this miserable body in order to see you without mediation,
O God, love, star of stars. In you, O dear love, I will be snatched
from the temptation of this death. Unworried and exultant, step-
ping over the wall of my body[56] into you, God, my lover, I will see
you there, in truth, face to face, without any obscurity.[57] 285

Ah! You fountain of sempiternal light, fetch me back into the
flow of your abyss from which I flowed forth (there where I may
recognize you just as I am recognized and love you just as I am
loved) so that forever I may see you, my God, as you really are[58] in
your blessed vision, fruition, and possession. Amen. 290

Also on this same day of love, you will offer your soul to the Lord
seven times[59] to freshen in yourself the love of his divine heart. And
first, at Lauds, pray the Lord himself, the supreme master, to teach
you the art of love[60] by the anointing of his Spirit, taking you up as
his own disciple, so that, with him as [your] teacher, you may be 295
exercised untiringly in the virtue of charity. And say:

Lord Jesus Christ, I have taken refuge in you; teach me to do
your will for you are my God.[61]

Prayer: O love, Rabbi, my Lord, sublimer than the heavens and
deeper than the abyss, whose wondrous wisdom blesses all things by 300
sight alone. From above the cherubs,[62] you look with fullest charity

---

55. Ps 15 (16):11.
56. Ps 17:30 (18:29).
57. 1 Co 13:12.
58. 1 Jn 3:2.
59. A reference to the canonical hours. We use the terms in accordance with the RB translation.
60. No doubt a reference to Ovid's *Ars amoris* which was wide-spread during the Middle
Ages.
61. Ps 142 (143):10.
62. Cf. Is 37:16.

upon things humble[63] in this valley of lamentation, and you bring
the children together for your saving dogmas. Ah! let your discipline
not pass over me, scum [that I am], but let your life-sustaining teach-
305   ing refresh me, I beseech you. If only, and a thousand times if only
you would adopt me as a daughter, to have and possess me as your
own. Ah! O love, begin now to exercise your mastery over me,
removing me from myself for the ministry of your living charity and
cherishing-love, O love, [and] possessing, sanctifying, and filling my
310   entire spirit. Amen.

At Prime, pray to the Lord to lead you into the school of love
where you may learn further to recognize and love Jesus. And [say]
this with prayer and verse:
        I am your handmaid, most loving Jesus; grant me the understand-
315   ing to learn your commandments.[64]
        O God, love, how well and how diligently you foster and nourish
your chicks in the bosom of charity. If only, and a thousand times if
only you would now open to me the school of chaste cherishing-
love that therein I might experience your dearest discipline and
320   through you be allotted a soul not only good[65] but, in truth, both
holy and perfect.
        Ah! O love, dip my senses in the marrow of your charity so that
through you I may become a gifted child and you yourself may be,
in truth, my Father, teacher, and master. And under your fatherly
325   blessing, let my spirit be wholly purified and refined from all the
scoria of sin. May it thus be given back, altogether fit—and apt to
capture your forgiving words. And may your holy, upright, and
foremost Spirit[66] dwell within all of me, O love. Amen.

330   At Terce, pray to the Lord to inscribe on your heart the fiery law
of his divine love with the living letters of his Spirit that you may

---

63. Ps 112:6 (113:7).
64. Ps 118 (119):73.
65. Cf. Ws 8:19.
66. Cf. Ps 50:12–14 (51:10–12).

cling to him inseparably at all hours. And [say] this with your prayer
and verse:

If only, most loving Jesus, all my thoughts and words and deeds
were directed to keep your justifications at all times.[67]   335

O God, love, how present you are to those seeking you. How
gentle, how dulcet to those finding you. Oh, if you now unfolded
your wondrous alphabet to me that my heart might enroll itself in
the same curriculum as you. Tell me now by living experience what   340
the glorious and foremost *alpha* of your beautiful cherishing-love is
like; and do not conceal from me that fruitful *beta* which fills genera-
tions with your imperial wisdom. Diligently and one by one, show
me with the finger[68] of your Spirit the individual letters of your   345
charity. Then reaching the very marrow of the foretaste of your
gentleness, let me, in truth, with the clean eye of my heart, scru-
tinize and examine, learn more, know and recognize them as wholly
as is lawful in this life.

Teach me through the co-operation of your Spirit the *tau* of supreme perfection and lead me to the *omega* of full consummation.[69]   350
In this life make me so perfectly learn more of your scripture,
[which is] full of charity and cherishing-love that in fulfilling your
charity not one *iota*[70] in me may be idle, for thereby I might endure
a delay when you, O God, love, my dulcet love, summon me to
you to contemplate you yourself in yourself forever. Amen.   355

At Sext, pray to the Lord that you may progress so much in the
art of loving him that his love may possess you as his own tool, as it
were, for all his will and that you be made entirely after God's own
heart. And say this prayer and verse:

Give me, my dear Jesus, true legislator, your most dulcet blessing   360
so that I may go from virtue to virtue and may see you, the God of
gods, in Sion.[71]

---

67. Ps 118 (119):5 and 20.
68. Lk 11:20.
69. Cf. Rv 1:8.
70. Mt 5:18.
71. Ps 83:8 (84:7).

O God, Love, everyone who does not cherish you is without a tongue and unable to speak: and only that one makes progress who, entirely clings to you, incessantly loving you alone. Ah! Let me not
365 always be left behind alone this way in the school of your charity, just like a tender chick of your rearing still in the egg; but let me in you and through you, by all means with you, advance and make progress from day to day, from virtue to virtue,[72] daily bearing fruit for you, my cherished one, on the new road of your cherishing-
370 love. And it is not sufficient for me to know you merely by syllables; I desire, I yearn for, and I earnestly wish a thousand times also to come to know you by theory,[73] to love you powerfully, not only dulcetly; but also to cherish you wisely and to cling inseparably to you, that I may begin now to live no longer in myself but in you
375 [and] for you alone. Now, O Love, make me recognize you in truth; and, in all holiness, set up a throne for you in my soul. Amen.

At None, pray to the Lord, the King of kings[74] himself, that he may accept you in the militia of love[75] and teach you to take upon yourself the pleasant yoke and light burden[76] so that you may fol-
380 low your Lord with your cross,[77] clinging to your God with undivided love; and [say] this with prayer and verse:

You, Lord, are my hope, my keeper, and my refuge: you are with me in every tribulation.[78]

---

72. Ibid.
73. Gertrud refers to the active and contemplative life. The active life is here represented by ability to spell, which implies familiarity with Scripture and other texts. The contemplative life is represented by theory and is the state she desires to progress to. Cf. also M. Déchanet, introduction to *The Golden Epistle*, XXXII., and cf. ExspSCh, 184, n. 4.
74. Rv 19:16; 1 Tm 6:15.
75. The *militia spiritualis*, here given as *militia amoris* and II, 387 as *dilectionis militia*, is a topos which has been traced back even to antique philosophy. Biblically, we find it in Jb 7:1 and then especially in St Paul, later in patristic literature. Gertrud may, in addition, have encountered the theme of 'spiritual combat' in RB, Prol. 3 and RB 2.20. Cf. also Hilarius Emonds, 'Geistlicher Kriegsdienst' in *Heilige Überlieferung*, ed. Odo Casel (Münster 1938) 21–56.
76. Mt 11:30.
77. Mk 8:34.
78. Ps 90 (91):2,15.

O God, cherishing-love, anyone who is found to be strong and
quick in the work of your love—that one truly will stand in the   385
presence of your royal face at all times. Ah! O queen of queens,
charity, make [me], for the sake of your glory, bound to you by
oath in the new militia of cherishing you. Teach me to set my hand
to strong things[79] and, in you and through you, quickly and unweariedly to go about and fulfill most faithfully the business of your   390
cherishing-love. Gird my thigh with the sword of your Spirit,[80]
most mighty one, and make me put on virility in my mind so that in
all virtue I may act viriliously and energetically; and, inseparably
with you, I may persevere, well strengthened in you,[81] with an unconquerable mind.

May all my vigor become so appropriated to your charity and my
senses so founded and firm in you that, while of the fragile sex, I   395
may, by virtue of a rational soul and virile mind, attain to that kind
of love which leads to the bridal-couch of the interior bed-chamber
of perfect union with you. Now, O love, hold and possess me as
your own, for already I no longer have—if not in you—either spirit   400
or soul. Amen.

At Vespers, march forward unworried, with Jesus, your lover, in
the armor of love against all temptation so that in him, whose mercy always aids and consoles you, you may be able to triumph over
your flesh, the world, and the devil, and to triumph gloriously over
every temptation. And demand this with prayer and verse: 405
My most dulcet Jesus, do not let my foot be moved, for you who
guard my soul neither sleep nor doze.[82]
O God, love, you alone are my wall and rampart.[83] Those who

---

79. Pr 31:19.
80. Eph 6:17; Ps 44:4 (45:3).
81. Given the context of repetitions of 'virility' and of military vocabulary, one might
wonder whether Gertrud intended a pun on *bene solidata*. Instead of 'well strengthened', the
phrase could be translated as 'the female/woman soldier' (from *solidatus* which means 'soldier,
mercenary').
82. Ps 120 (121):3-4.
83. Is 26:1.

410   bear distress in this world, behold, they know what kind of shelter
there is for them in your peace as a defense against heat and as a
canopy against rain.[84] Ah! Look upon and see my battle; you
yourself teach my hands to fight.[85] If armies in camp should stand
together against me, my heart will not fear[86] if you yourself, O my
415   faithful bulwark and strongest tower, were with me inside and outside.

Where is my opponent when you aid me? If you stand with me,
let him approach me here. By your sight alone, you lay open to me
and lay bare the thoughts of Satan, and, with a word, blow them
420   away in my presence. If my enemy throw me down headlong a
thousand times, in falling on your dearest right hand I will embrace
and kiss [it] warmly with all my heart; and, with you as a bulwark
and defense, I will stand undefiled, strong against all danger.

In me you crush Satan underfoot[87] and bring to naught and utter-
425   ly cause to flee all kinds of my defects. Under your gaze, may a
thousand fall at my side and a thousand thousand at my right
hand.[88] But let no evil approach me when you yourself are with me,
my supreme truth and dearest good. If only, and a thousand times if
430   only your sharp arrows[89] were at last turned toward me so that,
struck by the lance of your cherishing-love in my viscera, I might, O
charity, dwell with exceeding trust[90] in your midst and in you. Let
me already now, O love, fall here under you in such a way that for
eternity I may not slip from your hands. Amen.

At Compline, earnestly wish with the cherished one to become
435   inebriated[91] with the wine of love and in union with God to
become unconscious to the world; in the embrace of the cherished

---

84. Is 4:6.
85. Ps 143 (144):1.
86. Ps 26 (27):3.
87. Rm 16:20.
88. Ps 90 (91):7.
89. Ps 44:6 (45:5).
90. Jr 23:6.
91. Cf. Sg 1:3(4); 2:4.

one to expire from yourself into God; and already almost totally
stripped of [your] humanness, to go pleasantly to sleep on the breast
of Jesus.[92] Thus, dying daily to yourself in love and living for God
alone, you may, at the hour of death, trustfully run up to death,
looking on it as the end of your exile, the door of the kingdom, and   440
the gate of heaven. And [say] this with prayer and verse:

Hide me, most loving Jesus, in the hiding-place of your face[93]
from all those plotting crafty devices against me, and let my soul not
be confounded when it speaks with its enemies at the gate;[94] but fill
it full of gladness[95] with your mellifluous face.   445

O God, love, you are the consummation and the end of all good:
to the very end, you cherish[96] what you choose; whatever comes into your hand, you do not toss out[97] but preserve most diligently for
yourself. Ah! By right of possession make all my being and my con-   450
summation's end your own forever. Spare me now no longer, but
wound my heart[98] to the spirit's very marrow until you leave no
spark of life within me. Rather, take away with you my entire life,
reserving for yourself my soul in you.

Who will grant me to be consummated in you, O charity, and to   455
be delivered by your death from the prison of this body and to be
freed from this sojourn? How good, O love, to see you, have you,
and possess you for eternity. On the day I depart this life, may you
yourself be present, regardful of great consolation, and may you
bless me then in the beautiful dawn of the manifest contemplation   460
of you. Now, O love, I here leave you behind and commend to you
my life and, at the same time, my soul: allow me, allow me now to
rest and fall asleep in you in peace.[99] Amen.

---

92. See note 46.
93. Ps 30:21 (31:20).
94. Ps 126 (127):5.
95. Ps 15 (16):11.
96. Jn 13:1.
97. Jn 6:37.
98. Sg 4:9.
99. Ps 4:9 (8).

465   Also during that day when you are at leisure for love (for the kindling of your senses by the true sun, who is God, so that your love may never be extinguished but may grow from day to day) assiduously reflect on one of these verses:

Blessed the eyes that see you, O God, love.[100]

470   When, oh when may I come to that place where you are, God, true light, God and Lamb? I know that I will at last see you with my eyes,[101] O Jesus, my saving God.

Blessed are the ears that hear you, O God, love,[102] Word of life.

When, oh when will your voice full of mellifluous pleasantness console me, calling me to you?

475   Ah! Let me not fear hearing evil,[103] but let me quickly hear the glory of your voice.[104] Amen.

Blessed the nose that breathes you, O God, love, life's most dulcet aroma.

When, oh when will the fragrance of your mellifluous divinity breathe upon me?

480   Ah! Let me come quickly to the fat and lovely pastures of sempiternal vision of you. Amen.

Blessed the mouth that tastes, O God, love, the words of your consolation, sweeter than honey and the honeycomb.[105]

When, oh when will my soul be filled again out of the cream[106] of your divinity and become inebriated with your plentiful voluptuousness?[107]

485   Ah! Let me taste you thus *here*, my Lord, for you are pleasant[108] that *there* I may for eternity happily and thoroughly enjoy you, O God of my life. Amen.

---

100. Lk 10:23.
101. Cf. Jb 19:27.
102. Cf. Mt 13:15.
103. Ps 111 (112):7.
104. Cf. Ps 25 (26):7.
105. Ps 18:11 (19:10).
106. Ps 62:6 (63:5).
107. Ps 35:9 (36:8).
108. Ps 33:9 (34:8).

Blessed the soul that clings inseparably to you in an embrace of
love and
blessed the heart that senses the kiss of your heart,
O God, love, entering with you into a contract of friendship that
cannot be dissolved.

When, oh when will I be held tight in your blessed arms and   490
behold you, O God of my heart, without mediation?
Ah! Quickly, quickly, let me, snatched from this exile, in jubilation see your mellifluous face! Amen.

Finally, for the confirmation of love, give yourself up and resign
yourself altogether to the power of love, altogether clinging to God,   495
your lover, that he may have you as a tool for all the delight of his
divine heart and that, for himself, he preserve you in himself and
himself in you into eternal life. And say this prayer:
With love I hold you, most loving Jesus, nor shall I let you go;[109]
because your blessing is by no means sufficient for me[110] unless I   500
may hold you yourself and have my best share,[111] all my hope and
expectation. And, O love, life-giving life in the living Word of God,
which you yourself are, give me life, healing in me through you
whatever of God's love has been torn apart and extinguished.
O God, love, who have created me, recreate me in your love.   505
O love, who have redeemed me, whatever I have neglected of
your love, amend for yourself and redeem in me.
O God, love, who with the blood of your Christ have ransomed[112] me for yourself, sanctify me in your truth.[113]
O God, love, who have adopted me as a daughter, nourish, nour-   510
ish me after your own heart.
O love, who have chosen me for yourself and for no one else,
make me, all of me, cling to you.

---

109. Sg 3:4.
110. Cf. Gn 32:26 (28).
111. Lk 10:42.
112. Ac 20:28.
113. Jn 17:17.

O God, love, who have cherished me gratuitously, grant that I may cherish you with all my heart, all my soul, all my virtue.[114]
O love, most almighty God, embolden me in your love.

515 O wisest love, grant I may love you wisely.
O most dulcet love, grant I may taste you pleasantly.
O dearest love, grant I may live for you alone.
O most faithful love, console and aid me in every tribulation.
O most companionable love, work all my works in me.[115]

520 O most victorious love, grant I may persevere in you to the very end.

O love very close to my heart, who have never forsaken me, to you I commend my spirit.[116]

At the hour of death, receive me into yourself, calling me to you with your own mouth, saying: Today you will be with me.[117] Now
525 come forth from exile to the solemn *tomorrow* of unfading eternity. There you will find me, Jesus, the true *today* of divine brightness, who am the beginning and the end[118] of all creation. And for you no longer will a *tomorrow* follow in this mutability; but in me, the true *today*, you will have a sempiternal *today*, so that just as I live you may live in me, Jesus, God, your lover, in the happiest exulta-
530 tion without end. Let all forces, senses and movements of my body and soul say Amen.

---

114. Lk 10:27.
115. Is 26:12.
116. Lk 23:46 and Ps 30:6 (31:5)..
117. Lk 23:43.
118. Cf. Rv 1:8.

VI

JUBILUS[1]

NOW AND THEN, set aside for yourself a day on which, without hindrance, you can be at leisure to praise the divine and to make amends for all the praise and thanksgiving you have neglected all the days of your life to render to God for all the good he has done. And that will be a day of praising and thanksgiving and a day of jubilation, and you will celebrate the memory of that radiant praise with which you will be jubilant to the Lord for eternity, when you will be satisfied fully by the presence of the Lord; and your soul will be filled with the glory of the Lord.[2] (And for this reason mingled with these are devout deep sighs of the soul that strives to see the face of God. But among these praises are some so divine that they seem to belong to the blessed ones in their homeland rather than to those making their way on earth.)[3]

First, then, come to the face of your God in the spirit of humility in order that he may show you the grace of his countenance. And say:

I speak to my Lord, although I am dust and ashes.[4] O my God, exalted and sublime, look upon that which is humble far below;[5] my soul and my spirit grow faint at the limitless good you have done.

---

1. 'Exercise of Praise and Thanksgiving'.
2. 1 Kg 8:11.
3. The ExspSCh-editors are, no doubt, correct in assuming that the last two sentences are unlikely to have been written by Gertrud herself (201, n.6).
4. Gn 18:27.
5. Ps 112:6 (113:7).

Open to me the treasure of your most gracious heart, where the sum of my desires is stored. Open the grace of your mellifluous 20 countenance for me that I may pour out my soul under your gaze.[6] Open to me that most dulcet favor of my peace in you, which will exhilarate my soul and loosen my tongue in your praise.

Ah! O love, enter for me before the gaze of the great God and 25 there announce the clamoring of my desire because, in thirsting for God, all of my own virtue has already dried up. Ah, drag and draw my spirit upwards to you because already my flesh and my heart are growing faint[7] for God, my salvation. Ah! Present me to the Lord, my king, because my soul has already melted[8] with loving and 30 waiting for my spouse. O love, now very quickly fulfill my desire; if you delay I, already growing faint, will die for love.

At this point, start praising the Lord:

Rise up, my soul, rise up,[9] shake off the dust, lift yourself up, and 35 enter before the gaze of the Lord, your God, to confess before him all the mercy and compassion that he has shown to you. And what am I to the Lord, or how will I be able to answer him with one for a thousand?[10] O love, I endure violence; answer for me because I do not know what to say[11] to the God of my life. I have become 40 speechless in wonder at the glory of his countenance, and already I no longer have either voice or senses because my heart and virtue have withered away under the splendor of his majesty. O love— you, who are in God, my Jesus, Word of life—answer in my place; and on my behalf agitate this deified heart in which all your virtue 45 shines so visibly forth.

O love, while summoning [my] forces, let me say through you to

---

6. Cf. Ps 141:3 (142:2).
7. Ps 72 (73):26.
8. Sg 5:6.
9. Is 51:17 and 52:1.
10. Jb 9:3. The Bible context here speaks of one in a thousand arguments against God's justice.
11. Is 38:15.

the God of my salvation: You are the keeper of my soul.[12] You are
the life of my spirit. You are the God of my heart.[13] O love, play
most dulcetly on that very brightest lyre[14] of the throat of my
spouse Jesus so that he himself, God of my life, may on my behalf   50
sound the first voice[15] of praise for himself and may thus envelop
both my life and my soul in the delight of his praise. Ah! Now O
love, what you do, do quickly.[16] For already I am not capable of
bearing the serious wound you have inflicted on me.

At this point, arouse your soul to delight in God: 55
O my soul, now lift your eyes; look upon[17] and regard the might
of your king, the grace of your God, [and] the charity of your salva-
tion to which you have come near. Be at leisure now; taste and see[18]
how dulcet and how remarkable is the spouse whom you have
chosen above thousands.[19]
See what and how great is that glory for which you have con-   60
    demned the world.
See what that good is like for which you have waited.
See what the homeland is like for which you have sighed.
See what the prize is like for which you have labored.

---

12. Ps 53:6 (54:4).
13. Ps 72 (73):26.
14. The musical theme encountered throughout this chapter may be seen in close connection
with the Christ-Orpheus-theme, favored in art and literature since late antiquity. Specifically
the lyre, Orpheus' instrument, was the musical instrument to whose harmonies the soul 'was
believed to respond instinctively, . . . for this instrument was conducted according to the pattern of the universe, its seven strings corresponding to its seven spheres'. John Block Friedman,
Orpheus in the Middle Ages (Cambridge, Mass. 1970) 80.
15. 'First' is here used as a musical term, not as an adverb of normal speech. See also VI,
425.
16. Jn 13:27. ExspSCh rightfully draws attention to Gertrud's daring use of this text passage:
the words spoken by Jesus to Judas express Gertrud's own impatient love.
17. Cf. Jb 35:5.
18. Cf. Ps 45:11 (46:10). This psalm passage contains the alliterative combination of *vacare et
videre* (be still and see) which is frequent in Gertrud's text and in other spiritual writings of the
Middle Ages. Starting with *vacare* in this sentence, Gertrud adds the spiritual sense of *gustare*
(taste), as given in Ps 33:9 (34:8), and she then exploits the sense of sight anaphorically in the
following lines.
19. Sg 5:10.

See who your God is, what he is like and how great he is, whom
you have cherished, whom you have adored and for whom you
65   have always wished.
O God of my life, I do not know how I may worthily praise you
or with what I may reward you, my beloved, for all the good with
which you have rewarded me.[20] Consequently, I offer you in me,
and me in you, my cherished Jesus, as a holocaust of praise to you. I
70   have nothing further. This itself that I am and live in you, this I give
to you totally.[21]
You are my life. You are my sufficiency. You are my glory. You
are the proof of mercy that is resplendent in my soul. To you be
praise and supreme thanksgiving. Oh, when will I burn up the mar-
75   row of my soul on your altar and, in this holy fire that continuously
burns there, inflame my heart and immolate myself totally as a
sacrifice of praise to you.[22]
Ah! O God, my holy gentleness, widen my heart in you, and extend my soul in order that all my viscera may be filled with your
80   glory. Oh, when will my soul be told: Turn to your rest[23] because
the Lord has been the one to do you good? Oh, when will I hear
that merriest voice: Come, enter into the inner chamber of your
spouse? Oh, when will I rest and fall asleep[24] in you, Jesus, my most
dulcet peace, that I may see your glory?[25]
85   But you, O life of my spirit, are able to keep my deposit for me,[26]
and to lead my soul back to you who have created me. O love, love,
when will you lead my soul out of its prison? Oh, when will you
release me personally from the shackles of the body? When, O
when will you lead me into the inner chamber of my spouse that I
90   may be joined inseparably to him in fruition. Ah! O love, hasten my
nuptials because I wish to die a thousand times to be able to expe-

---

20. Ps 115 (116):12.
21. Ac 3:6.
22. Ps 115 (116):17.
23. Ps 114 (116):7.
24. Ps 4:9 (8).
25. Ps 62:3 (63:2).
26. 2 Tm 1:12.

rience such delights; I seek, however, not my convenience but your gracious purpose.

Then, as if growing faint with wonder at your God's glory, stand before his countenance, at which [even] the angels desire to 95 glimpse²⁷ and, greeting with these words the face of your God's glory, read with you heart and mouth the first psalm: Bless [the Lord].²⁸

Blessed are you, Adonai, in the firmament of heaven.²⁹
Let all the marrow and virtue of my spirit bless you.
Let all the substance of my soul and body bless you. 100
Let all that is within me glorify you.

Let all my desires be in jubilation together for you because you alone are praiseworthy and glorious forever.³⁰ Already my heart and my virtue have forsaken me,³¹ and the marrow of my spirit has gone after you, God, my lover, who created me for yourself. And my soul which you have redeemed,³² groaning because I am delayed 105 by my sojourn, mentally follows you into the sanctuary where you yourself, my king and my God, abide in the substance of my flesh.

Oh, how blessed [are] those who dwell in your house.³³ How most blessed those who stand in the presence of your mellifluous face. Truly, truly, they will praise you forever for your immense 110 glory. When, oh when will my soul go into the place of your wonderful tabernacle ³⁴ so that my mouth may praise you along with these most blessed ones, proclaiming in great merriment for eternity 'holy, holy, holy' before your mellifluous face?

Oh, how glorious you are, my God, how lovable, how praise- 115 worthy on the holy throne of your divinity. How exquisite is your light to the eyes. What a blessing [it is] to see you, the true sun. How radiant, how merry, how comely your praise where thou-

---

27. 1 Pt 1:12.
28. Ps 102 (103).
29. Dn 3:56.
30. Ibid.
31. Ps 37:11 (38:10).
32. Ps 70 (71):23.
33. Ps 83:5 (84:4).
34. Ps 41:5 (42–43:4).

120   sands and thousands stand before you.[35] There, leaping out of
myself into you, my living God, my heart and soul already exult.
Oh, how great is your glory, my God, my holy gentleness, in front
of the holy throne of your kingdom,[36] where all your angels and
saints praise you.

Behold, my soul already languishes and grows faint because of this
125   life's tediousness,[37] and with all my heart I yearn to be dissolved[38]
and to be with you. Then I, too, the scum[39] of all your creation,
may be able, among the ever-blessed bands that are jubilant in your
praise in the highest heaven, to offer you marrow-rich holocausts of
jubilation. There, on the golden altar of your divine heart, I will
130   burn up for you the dearest incense of my spirit and soul together
with the cream of your most pleasant anointing, the grand and great
gentleness, with which you yourself, my Father and Lord, have consoled me in all my tribulations and anxieties.[40]

135   At this point, break out in a voice of praise:
May all your miraculous works and all those most generous gifts
which I have from you, O God of my life, bless you, glorify you,
and magnify you on my behalf.

May your great compassion and grand mercy bless you, together
with the unlimited good you have done, by which, O God of my
140   heart, you have been the one to do good to my soul.

May all that is within me,[41] both my whole substance and virtue,
bless you because you are the God of my salvation, the keeper of
my soul.

At this point, you will be jubilant to the Lord before the throne of
145   God and the Lamb[42] on account of all his benefactions.

---

35. Dn 7:10.
36. Dn 3:54.
37. Ps 118 (119):28.
38. Cf. Ph 1:23.
39. 1 Co 4:13.
40. 2 Co 6:4.
41. Cf. Ps 102 (103):1.

May the desires of my very heart and my vows be jubilant to you, and let the gifts of your many graces confess you.

May the groans and sighs of my miserable sojourn be jubilant to you; and may that which you yourself are, my God—my long wait, patience, and expectation—bless you.

May my hope and trust in you be jubilant to you because, at last, 150 you will lead me back from dust[43] to you, O most blessed life, my God.

May the seal of faith, with which you have marked me out as yours, be jubilant to you because I believe that at last I may see you in my flesh,[44] O my dear redeemer.

May the desire I have for you and the thirst which I endured for you be jubilant to you because, after this life, I may at last come to you, O true homeland, my God.

May divine love, too, which, coming before my love, obliges me to love you incessantly, be jubilant to you above everything, because you, my God, my dulcet love, are alone God, blessed 160 forever.

At this point, you will worship before the face of the Lord, your God, praying with a devout heart and mouth that Jesus may make amends for you.

When, oh when, most loving Jesus, will I go into your house with holocausts[45] to offer to you there a vociferant sacrifice[46] and sur- 165 render to you those vows that my lips have uttered during my tribulation.[47]

When, oh when will I come and appear before your holy throne to see your mellifluous countenance whose divinest light in itself satisfies the desire of all the saints and turns their hearts together 170 with their voices and lips to dulcet jubilation.

---

42. Rv 22:1.
43. Cf. Jb 10:9.
44. Jb 19:25–26.
45. Ps 65 (66):13.
46. Ps 26 (27):6.
47. Ps 65 (66):13–14.

Ah! O cherished one of my vows, understand my cry.[48] Direct
your attention to my prayer and heed me; for the sigh of my heart
175   and the desire of my soul, O my king and my God, call you, want
you, and need you. Because of you my eyes drop tears, and my look
is intent on you. You alone my God, my gentleness and cherishing-
love, and my hope from my youth:[49] you yourself are all that I wish
for, hope for, and yearn for.

And now, O my cherished one, in that overpowering love in
180   which you are seated in my flesh at the right hand of the Father,
reserve me for yourself, inscribed in your hands[50] and feet and, at
the same time, on your most dulcet heart,[51] so that for eternity you
may not forget my soul which you have redeemed[52] so dearly. My
God, my mercy, now, for all the good that you have done, do, and
185   will do for me, render to yourself on my behalf the eternal, immense, and immutable praises that you are able to and [that you]
have power over in yourself and [that you] know to be congruous
with the most revered glory and honor of your majesty. Break out
for me, my dear Jesus, in a voice of such joyous thanksgiving as
190   becomes you, my Lord, ever great and miraculous. Praise yourself
in yourself, in me and for me, with all the virtue of your divinity,
with all the affection of your humanity, [and on behalf of] and with
the affection of all the universe until at length you lead me, an atom
of your universal creation, along through you, who are the way,
195   and lead me up to you, who are the truth, and lead me into you,
who are the life,[53] and hide me that your very dulcet face full of
grace may be my share for eternity.[54]

At this point, as if delighted and refreshed with wonder at God's

---

48. Ps 5:2 (1).
49. Ps 70 (71):5.
50. Cf. Is 49:16.
51. This passage may be understood as an allusion to Christ's wounds. Cf. ExspSCh, 214,
n. 2.
52. Ps 70 (71):23.
53. Cf. Jn 14:6.
54. Ps 72 (73):26.

glory, greet God, your lover, with these words by reading the heavenly psalm: I will extol you, God, my King.[55]   200
My king and my God—God, love and joy—my soul and my
heart are jubilant to you. My heart desires to greet, praise, magnify,
and bless you, life of my soul, my God—God living and true, fountain of sempiternal light, the light of whose mellifluous face has   205
marked me, an unworthy woman. I offer to you the marrow of my
forces and of my senses as a holocaust of new praise and intimate
thanksgiving.

And with what will I reward you, my Lord, for all the good with
which you have rewarded me?[56] Behold, as I see it, you have cher-   210
ished me above your glory, and for my sake you have not spared
yourself. To this end you have created me for you, and you have
redeemed me for yourself and have chosen me, that you may lead
me right up to you and grant that I live in blessedness in you and
enjoy you most happily for eternity. For what is there for me in
heaven now other than you, or what more of all your good do I   215
wish or yearn for apart from you?[57]

My Lord, you are my hope; you the glory; you the joy; you my
blessedness. You are the thirst of my spirit; you the life of my soul,
you the jubilation of my heart. Where above you could my wonder
lead me, my God? You are the beginning and the consummation of   220
all the good, and in you all those who are glad have, as it were, a
dwelling-place together. You are the praise in my heart and mouth.
You glow altogether red in the spring-like loveliness of the festival of
your love. May your most outstanding divinity magnify and glorify
you because you are the source of light and the fountain of life forever.[58] No creature suffices to praise you worthily. You alone are   225
sufficient to yourself who are never deficient in yourself. Your face,
mellifluous above honey and the honeycomb,[59] fattens the souls of
saints.

---

55. Ps 144 (145).
56. Ps 115 (116):12.
57. Ps 72 (73):25.
58. Ps 35:10 (36:9).
59. Ps 18:11 (19:10).

At this point, bless the Lord God, your great king, for all his com-
230   passion:

May your glorious and wondrous light, my God, bless you for
me, and may the imperial comeliness of your most outstanding
majesty praise you.

May the worthiest magnificence of your immense glory bless
you, and may the very brightest virtue of your unlimited might
praise you.

235   May the foremost sunshine of your eternal brightness bless you,
and may your red-glowing and lovely comeliness, flashing like light-
ning, praise you.

May the abyss of your just judgments bless you, and may the in-
scrutable encompassing of eternal wisdom praise you.

240   May the unlimited acts of your great compassion bless you, and
may the immense weight of all your mercy praise you.

At this point, offer the sacrifice of jubilation, saying devoutly:

May all the viscera of your loving-kindness and the superabun-
245   dant copiousness of your unlimited goodness be jubilant to you.

May your exceedingly great and overflowing charity, which you
have toward humankind, and the unrestrained liberality of your
most gracious love be jubilant to you.

May the triumphant strength of your overflowing gentleness and
the fullness of all your blessedness that abides in you for those dear
250   to you be jubilant to you.

At this point, adore the Lord God,[asking] that he may lead you
quickly into his holy tabernacle and that he may praise himself for
you, and say these words:

O most blessed life, my God, upon whom alone my eyes look.
255   When, oh when will your life-sustaining ray draw me back and
draw me, the least spark, into the splendors of the saints[60] so that,
also on my tongue, the jubilation of your praise may resound before

---

60. Ps 109 (110):3.

your throne, where equal praise from everyone is given to God the
Father and the Son and the Holy Spirit in one dulcet rhythm of
thanksgiving. Oh, when will the strings of my desire be fitted onto   260
those seraphic lutes that without cease proclaim to you the ineffable
'holy', so that in your presence the joy and jubilation of my heart
may sound in unison with the blessed ones [in singing] that same
praise.

Oh, when, [once] I have been snatched from the snares of the   265
hunters,[61] will your snow-white, spotless fleece enfold me so that I
may see you, an exemplar of radiance exceeding the countenance of
angels, going before the choruses of virgins and saints? And when
may I hear the new song of the eternal marriage, which you, O
their king and spouse, play before them so dulcetly on the cithara?
This is the song in which the glory of your clearest voice sounds   270
above all the cymbals of heaven, in which every voice and tongue
grow faint before this praise that is so worthy of you yourself.[62]

Oh how cheerful is the jubilation where the supreme and eternal
voice of praise and thanksgiving sound in unison to the one and   275
triune Lord from the one and triune deity, where, putting its comeliness aside, all the heavenly music falls silent; and [where] all the
company of seraphim fold their wings. Ah! O God of my heart and
cherished one of my vows. There, there in the self-sufficiency that
you have from that fullest abundance of yourself for me, an unwor-   280
thy woman, at this hour, in the jubilation of your divine heart, add
to your voice a new melodious round of praise and thanksgiving.
And for me, may the vocal organ of your jubilation give you satisfaction for all the good you have done in creating, redeeming, and
choosing me from the world.   285

Ah, and in this melodious round of praise, include my cherishing-
love for you by such an indivisible knot of love that the marrow of
my heart may, unweariedly, be jubilant to you. All the while I bear
my miserable sojourn, I will always thirst to praise you and yearn to
return to you who have created me—until, having put aside this   290

---

61. Ps 123 (124):7.
62. Christ is seen here both as the cithara player and the singer (see also VI, 425 f.).

heap of flesh, I appear in the sanctuary in your presence. There, under the aspect of your divinest countenance, my heart may be filled again with joy and my tongue with jubilation:[63] there I may exult forever because of your goodness and glory in the sempiternal fruition of your mellifluous face. Amen.

295   At this point as if almost melted away and drained of life before the immensity of the riches and delights of the glory of your God, by the inestimable beauty of his praise, by the glory of those standing around him, and by the mellifluous radiance of his most splendid and glorious countenance, invite all creation to praise God
300   with the hymn 'Bless the Lord all you works of the Lord'[64] and with this prayer:

My heart and my flesh have exulted in you, my living God,[65] and my soul has been gladdened by you, my true salvation. Oh how wondrous is your temple, God, king of virtues. How glorious your
305   dwelling-place, where you, God most high, preside in your majesty over all things. The virtue of my soul grows faint in its yearning to enter into your glory. God, my God, love and jubilation of my heart, refuge and virtue,[66] God, my glory and my praise, oh when will my soul praise you in the church of the saints?[67]
310   Oh when will my eyes see you, my God, God of gods? God of my heart, oh when will you gladden me with the sight of your mellifluous face? Oh when will you bestow upon me the desire of my soul by manifesting your glory? My God, my choicest portion, my strength
315   and glory. Oh when will I enter into your might[68] to see your virtue and glory?[69] Oh when will you clothe me with the mantle of your praise instead of a spirit of sorrow so that, together with the angels, all the parts of my body may render you a vociferant sacrifice.[70]

---

63. Ps 125 (126):2.
64. Dn 3:57. The entire canticle (Dn 3:57–88) is still used in the Sunday Lauds of the Divine Office.
65. Ps 83:3 (84:2).
66. Ps 45:2 (46:1).
67. Ps 149:1.
68. Ps 70 (71):16.
69. Ps 62:3 (63:2).
70. Ps 26 (27):6.

God of my life, oh when will I enter into the tabernacle of your
glory in order that I, too, may proclaim to you the most splendid   320
alleluia and that my soul and my heart may confess to you in the
presence of all your saints that you have magnified your mercies
toward me.[71] My God, my very bright inheritance, oh when, after
the snares of this death have been destroyed, will I personally see
you without mediation, and praise you? Oh when will I dwell in   325
your tabernacle forever[72] in order that I may assiduously praise
your name and sing to your magnificence a new hymn about your
multitudinous mercies?

There is none among the gods like you,[73] my Lord, nor is there
anything equal to the lofty riches of your wondrous glory. Who   330
will search into the abyss of your wisdom, and who will count out
the unlimited treasures of your most copious mercy? Truly, nothing
is as wondrous as you, my God, immortal king, nothing as glorious.
Who will unfold the glory of your majesty? Who will [ever] be able
to be sated with the sight of your brightness? How will the eye suf-   335
fice to see or the ear to hear in wondering at the glory of your
countenance?

God, my God, you alone are wondrous and glorious. You alone
are great and praiseworthy, alone dulcet and lovable, alone beautiful
and lovely, alone radiant and full of delight. And you alone are so   340
wondrous and glorious; your equal is not found in all the glory of
heaven and earth. For my heart, your wondrous light[74] is lovable
above all glory because it alone can bring gladness to my spirit and
exchange the tediousness of this life for exultation and joy.   345

Oh, when will you inextinguishably light the oil lamp of my soul
and rekindle it in you so that, as I am recognized, I may recognize
myself in you?[75] Oh how happy, how blessed those who are already
kept hidden within the glory of your countenance. Oh, when will

---

71. Gn 19:19.
72. Ps 60:5 (61:4).
73. Ps 85 (86):8; 1 Ch 17:20.
74. 1 Pt 2:9.
75. Cf. 1 Co 13:12—This appears to be one of Gertrud's favorite New Testament passages.
She often quotes *facie ad faciem* (face to face); here she refers to *cognoscam sicut et cognitus sum*,
but adapting it to her feminine perspective.

350	that most dulcet ray also absorb me, an unworthy woman, so that I
	may become one love and one spirit with you? All that is within me
	says to you: Lord, who is like you?[76] Truly, you have no equal in
	glory because you alone are God, glorified and exalted above all for
	ever.[77] Oh, when will you raise this pauper from the dust; when
355	may I stand before your royal face? Instead of ashes you will give me
	the crown of everlasting joy so that my soul, with a voice of sem-
	piternal jubilation, may render praise to you for all the good that
	you have with such grace bestowed on me.[78]

	My soul and my heart already seethe for you, God of my heart,
360	and the God that is my share for eternity.[79] In you my spirit exults,
	O God, my salvation.[80] If all creation were within my power I
	would unite all things in the glory of your praise; and all the very
	bright works of your fingers.[81] Now remembering your praise,[my]
	mind and soul melt. If I had the force of all angels and human be-
365	ings,[82] I would expend it readily and freely in your praise, that it
	might be given to me to see how copious are the eulogies of praise
	and joyful homage before your holy throne, where you observe the
	sabbath in a most blessed rest, you and the ark of your holiness with
370	you,[83] and where day and night thousands of thousands stand
	before you[84] proclaiming 'holy, holy, holy' without ceasing.

	There, there, into the golden censer of your divine heart, where
	the most pleasant aromatic thyme of eternal love continuously
	burns up in your praise, I also throw the minutest grain of my heart.
375	I yearn for and desire that it, too, my vile and unworthy heart,
	made passionately alive through the breath of your Spirit, may
	cross over into the one brazier of your praise, and that the deep
	sighs for you (which, because of my long expectation I draw from

---

76. Ps 34 (35):10.
77. Dn 3:52.
78. Ps 115 (116):12.
79. Ps 72 (73):26.
80. Lk 1:47.
81. Ps 8:4 (3).
82. Cf. I Co 13:1.
83. Ps 131 (132):8.
84. Dn 7:10.

the abyss of the earth) may be everlasting praise and glory to you.
Amen.

Then, as if transported in spirit and soul in God's praise and not   380
finding words comparable with his worthiness, pray to the Lord
Jesus, your lover, to glorify himself for you with praise of such
worth as becomes him, as pleases him, and as he himself most
delights in being praised with. And say with a devout heart and
mouth:

May the holy divinity of your glory, my God, O my gentleness,   385
with which you deigned to fill and to inhabit for nine months the
chaste viscera of the Virgin Mary, bless you.

May the highest virtue of your divinity, which bent to the
humbleness of the virginal valley, bless you.

May the utmost art of your almightiness, God most high, with   390
which you imparted onto the virgin rose such virtue, radiance, and
comeliness as you yourself could yearn for, bless you.

May your wondrous wisdom, whose copious grace made all of
Mary's life and body as well as her soul comparable with your worthiness, bless you.

May your strong, wise, and most dulcet love which made you,   395
the flower and spouse of virginity, become the Son of a virgin, bless
you.

May the emptying of your majesty, which ransomed the treasures
of eternal inheritance for me, bless you.

May your assumption of our humanity, which called me to consort with your divinity, bless you.

May your exile, which you endured for me for thirty-three years   400
so that you might lead my soul (which had perished) back to the
fountain of eternal life, bless you.

May all the labor, pain and sweat of your humanity, with which
you have made holy all my anxieties, distress, and languor, bless
you.

May the experience of my misery, through which you have   405
become for me the Father of much mercy and God of unlimited
clemency, bless you.

May your copious cherishing-love, through which you yourself have become the precious redemption of my soul, bless you.

410   May each and every drop of your most precious blood, with which you have given life to my soul and have so dearly redeemed me, bless you.

May the bitterness of your precious death, which your strong love has inflicted on you for me, bless you. By right [of your death] I am not confounded by taking for my own use from you whatever

415   I lack in merits of my own, or by presuming and knowing that you truly care for me—for you are mine and I am yours by the perpetual right of [your] having personally ransomed me forever.

May your triumphant glory, by which you are seated in my flesh at the right hand of the Father, bless you for me—God blessed forever.

420   May your own brightness, honor, and virtue, with which all the heavenly hosts are miraculously filled again and nourished, bless you.

At this point, as if, all of you, clinging to God, your lover, pray to the Lord that he himself with his much beloved genitrix, the Virgin Mary, and with all the heavenly militia, offer himself as a sacrifice of jubilation in the cheerful festival of his merriest love; and that he

425   himself, the most dulcet cithara player, sing first with the vocal organ of his divinity and with the cithara of his humanity. Then say these words with heart and mouth:

May, the divinity of your imperial Trinity, your essential unity,

430   the uniqueness of your persons, their dulcet fellowship, and their mutual intimate familiarity be jubilant to you on my behalf, God of my life.

May the sublimity of your incomprehensible worthiness, your immutable eternity, your uncontaminated purity, the fountain of your holiness, and your glorious and perfect happiness be jubilant to you.

May the cleanest flesh of your humanity, in which you cleansed

435   me, having been made bone of my bones, and flesh of my flesh,[85] be jubilant to you.

---

85. Gn 2:23.

May your very brightest soul, that most precious pledge with which my soul was redeemed, be jubilant to you.

May your mellifluous and deified heart, which love broke in death for me, be jubilant to you.

May your most gracious and most faithful heart (into which the lance made a way for me so that, entering into it, my heart might   440
there repose) be jubilant to you.

May that most dulcet heart, the only refuge during my sojourn (which is so lovingly-kind and always solicitous of me and will never rest in thirsting for me until at length it receives me forever to itself) be jubilant to you.

May the worthiest heart and soul of the most glorious Virgin   445
Mother Mary (whom, because of my need for salvation, you chose for yourself as mother and that her motherly clemency might always be open to me) be jubilant to you on my behalf.

May that most faithful concern which is yours for me (by which you have provided me with an advocate and patron saint of such capability that through her I may easily be able to find your grace, and in whom, I trustfully believe, your eternal mercy is preserved   450
for me) be jubilant to you.

May that wonderful tabernacle[86] of your glory, which alone has ministered to you worthily as a holy dwelling-place and through which you can best make amends for me to yourself for the due measure of praise and glory that I owe you, be jubilant to you.

May the seven glorious spirits, who stand gazing before your   455
throne,[87] be jubilant to you on my behalf.

May the unlimited camps of holy angels, whom you sent in ministry for the sake of the chosen race[88] you have ransomed, be jubilant to you.

May the twenty-four elders[89] with all the patriarchs and prophets (who, putting aside their crowns, prostrate themselves before your   460

---

86. Ps 41:5 (42–43:4).
87. Rv 1:4.
88. 1 Pt 2:9.
89. Rv 5:8.

throne, rendering unlimited praises and thanksgiving to you on citharas) be jubilant to you.

May the four winged holy animals all of whose viscera belch forth your praise day and night,[90] be jubilant to you.

465   May the apostolic worthiness of your best friends, your brothers, through whose petitions you miraculously uphold your holy church, be jubilant to you.

May the victorious company of martyrs, whose retinue is empurpled with your most precious blood,[91] be jubilant to you.

May the band of your most perfect confessors, whose spirit you
470   have transported into your wondrous light,[92] be jubilant to you.

May all the holy and spotless virgins, who, one with you, are adorned with the brightness of the same snow-white purity, be jubilant to you.

May that new song, which resounds from their mouths when they follow you wherever you go, good Jesus, king and spouse of virgins,[93] be jubilant to you on my behalf.

475   May the marrow of your divinity and the cream of your gentleness, with which the heavenly Jerusalem[94] is sated and fattened in the splendor of your divine countenance, be jubilant to you on my behalf.

May all the army of your chosen (share of your inheritance and special people because they are with you and you are with them,
480   their God for eternity) be jubilant to you.

May all the stars of heaven (which glow with gladness for you and which, having been called to order by you, are always ready to stand by you[95]) be jubilant to you.

May all your miraculous works, whatever is grasped within the circumference of heaven, earth, and the abyss, be jubilant to you
485   and forever give you that praise which, going out from you, flows back into you, its source.[96]

---

90. Rv 4:8.
91. Cf. Rv 7:14.
92. 1 Pt 2:9.
93. Rv 14:3–4.
94. Cf. Is 66:10.
95. Cf. Ba 3:33–35.
96. *Legatus* II (139) 23, 8f. ends with a very similar passage.

May my heart and soul with all the substance of my flesh and spirit, through the efficacy of the entire universe, be jubilant to you. To you, then, from whom everything, through whom everything, and in whom everything, to you alone [be] honor and glory forever. Amen.

Then, as if you were somewhat refreshed by praising your God,   490
your king, who is in the sanctuary, rise up now with heart wide open to delight in God, your lover, throwing into him all the love of your heart so that *here* he may nourish you with the blessing of his gentleness[97] and *there* may lead you to the blessing of his plenitude of fruition forever. And [say] this with these words: 495
God, my God, because you are mine I lack nothing.[98] And because I am yours, I will glory in you, God, my savior,[99] for eternity. In all my sadness, you prepare for me in you the banquets of homage. And where is my soul's well-being if not in you, O God of my life? If the memory of your praise is so dulcet in this misery,   500
what will it be like, my God, when in the splendor of your divinity your glory appears? If the small drops of this foretaste of you are so refreshing, what will it be like, my holy dulcet one, when you are given to me copiously? If you console me here by fulfilling my desire with good things, what will it be like, O God of my salvation,   505
when you absorb my spirit in you?

Oh how rich will be the pastures of the intimacy of your mellifluous face when, admitted to the pastures of your gentleness here, (in, alas, an hour rare and for a moment brief)[100] my soul, having melted, may thus pass over into you. Oh what will be the refresh-   505
ment in the presence of your divine countenance when [even] here, at the waters of internal refreshment, you so merrily and so pleasantly nourish the marrow of my spirit and soul. God, my God,

---

97. Ps 20:4 (21:3).
98. Ps 22 (23):1.
99. Lk 1:47.
100. This phrase is a direct quote from St Bernard, SC 23.15: 'Alas! how rare the time, and how short the stay!' (Cf. ExspSCh,237, n. 6). The identical phrase is also found in Aelred of Rievaulx, De Iesv pvero', *Opera omnia* (CCCM 1), eds. A. Hoste and C. H. Talbot (Turnholt 1971) 270; 11. 148–149.

when you turn my soul to you, you do not allow me either to think
or to sense anything but you, and you take me away from myself
515   into you so that nothing can be of concern to me because you hide
me from myself in you.

And then, what joy there will be, what exultation, what jubilation when you open to me the comeliness of your divinity and my
soul sees you face to face?[101] Surely, then, there is nothing I would
520   more willingly do than be at leisure and see[102] your glory, God, and
circle the altar of my reconciliation, and immolate the marrow of
my soul for you in jubilation and praise.

Then, O my soul, you will see and rush forward and your heart
will marvel and open wide[103] when the multitude of riches and of
525   delights and the magnificence of the glory of that great ocean of the
entire and always venerable Trinity are turned to you; when the
strength of nations (that the King of kings and Lord of lords[104] with
a strong hand redeemed for himself from the hand of the enemy)
comes to you; when the inundation of divine mercy and charity,
530   almightiness, wisdom, and goodness covers you with your lot: eternal adoption.

Then will be presented to you the chalice of vision, the inebri-
ating and very bright chalice[105] of the glory of the divine countenance; and you will drink from the torrent of divine voluptuousness,[106] and you will become inebriated when the fountain of light
535   itself refreshes you eternally in the delights of its fullness. Then you
will see the heavens full of the indwelling glory of God and that
virginal light giver—that, after God, lights up the entire heaven with
the brightness of its cleanest light—and the miraculous works of the
fingers of God, and the morning stars that always so merrily stand
540   before the face of God, ministering to him.[107]

---

101. 1 Co 13:12.
102. Ps 45:11 (46:10).
103. Is 60:5.
104. Rv 19:16; 1 Tm 6:15.
105. Cf. Lm 4:21; Ps 22 (23):5.
106. Ps 35:9 (36:8).
107. Jb 38:7; cf. Tb 12:15.

O God of my heart and my choicest portion,[108] alas, alas, how long, how long will my soul be barred from the presence of your most dulcet countenance? You alone sufficiently acknowledge all the misery of my sojourn; you know how fragile it is, and how deep is the misery of the exile in which I live. 545

Ah! O cherished one of my vows, my innermost heart thirsts for you.

Ah! Quickly make me come to you, God, living fountain;[109] from you let me draw eternal life forever.

Ah! Quickly let your face shine upon me;[110] let me gladly see you face to face.[111]

Ah! Quickly, quickly show yourself to me; let me rejoice happily 550 in you for eternity.

Ah! ah! O life of my spirit, transport the cry of my desire and join it in one voice with the festive psaltery of your love. And make my life so much your own and glue my soul to your love in such a way that all my life and acts may sing praise to you on the ten-string 555 psaltery[112] and that my total intention united to you, may commence, progress, and terminate in you, O true life of my soul.

Ah! and ah! O true love of my heart, at this hour render to yourself on my behalf such solemn and such very bright comeliness of 560 praise and thanksgiving that all the heavenly order may join in jubilation for that ever-greatest and most dulcet good which you are for me, my God, and for your deigning to be acknowledged, loved, and praised by me, scum of all your creation. For you are my saving God, the entire cause of my salvation and the life of my soul. 565

Ah, and in the comeliness of this praise, let my soul expend on you the trifling speck of my spirit's marrow until the time that my spirit, melting for love in your praise, happily goes back to you, God. Ah, and in this life, give me such delight in the memory of 570 your praise that at the hour of my death my thirst for seeing you,

---

108. Ps 72 (73):26.
109. Ps 41:3 (42–43:2)
110. Ps 30:17 (31:16).
111. 1 Co 13:12.
112. Ps 143 (144):9.

praising you, and being with you together may, with my strong love, triumph over the force of death. And, in order that my spirit and soul may for eternity exult in you, may you yourself be for me the gate and homeland in that anxiety until the time when you lead
575   me to the intimate joys of heavenly life. Amen.

Then (like a lonely turtle dove) growing faint because of the weariness of this life in your eagerness to see the mellifluous face of your cherished one[113] and lowering the wings of your desires (with the holy animals before God's throne[114]), profess in the presence of
580   the Lord, your God, that your heart is entirely there where he himself is your desirable treasure;[115] and entreat from him a happy passing away.

My heart sticks fast there where Jesus, my life, wills it to be. Ah! Jesus, cherished before all cherished ones, you are the faithful life of my soul. You are the total languor of my soul: for you alone thirsts
585   my innermost heart. Your delightful blessedness, your miraculous beauty, your honorable image, [and] your lovable radiance have fixed within me a very pleasant wound—because of which, seeing the light of this world weighs me down.

I am weary of myself. How long, how long must I wait, O my
590   cherished one, to enjoy you, and to contemplate your lovable face? You are the thirst of my soul. Heaven, earth, and everything that is in them are like a winter frost without you. Your lovable face is my only consolation, a spring solace.

595   O love, love, when will you give me this gift: that my body having been slain by you may turn back to dust, and my soul may flow back into you, God, its living source? Your purest divine outpourings, which so lovably shine forth from your highest throne in their god-
600   like rays, powerfully seize all my spirit. What more shall a little tree leaf wait for in such a powerful storm of this age?

Ah, love, love, hold me in your mighty right hand lest my soul be

---

113. Cf. Sg 2:12–14.
114. Cf. Rv 5:11.
115. Mt 6:21.

overwhelmed by it. The dulcet sound of living water, flowing out of the source itself, has powerfully captured my heart: ah, never has any lyre made so dulcet a sound. This life, like a dream,[116] has become vile for me. How long, how long will I endure its illusion? Ah, love, love, never deliver me from your bond until at length you present me to the one and only cherished one of my heart, in   610 his most dulcet bosom. Dulcet scent of the fruit of life, which you yourself are, my especially cherished one, you have led my spirit away from me, and now my rotten body stinks like a dung pit to me,[117] wherefore I will never cease to sigh for you.

Ah, love, love, when will you deliver me from my body so that,   615 without mediation, I may fully enjoy the cherished one of my heart and abide with him without limit. The one and only ray of your divinity standing out to me through your humanity miraculously gladdens my spirit, so that if I had a thousand bodies, I would quickly contemn them. What delights, then, may lie hidden in the fruition   620 of your brightness [when it is made] transparent? A thousand deaths would be nothing to me if I were permitted to contemplate the gentleness of your truth.

Ah, love, love, treat me mercifully, and lift me quickly up to that renowned festival where I may contemplate the glory of the faithful   625 savior, my spouse. Only the fullness of your divinity can satisfy my soul, which you deigned to create for yourself. Imbibing only one drop of your gentleness ravishes my spirit so powerfully that, over all life, I inwardly savor death through which I might contemplate your face continually.   630

Ah, love, love, when will you so separate my soul from my body that my spirit may dwell assiduously in you, my dearest one? Your lovable embrace has such a dulcet savor that if I had a thousand hearts they would quickly melt. Your lively kiss submerges my life   635 in you and strongly ties my mind to you. How willingly, how will-

---

116. Contrary to frequent biblical and other medieval usage, Gertrud in this text employs *somnium* (dream) only in the negative sense of 'idle whim'. Cf. also VII, 139.

117. This is language with which Gertrud may have been familiar from the Psalms (see, e.g., 112 (113):7) and from Bernard, SC, such as 7.7, 24.5–7 [passim], 35.5, and especially 40.1 ('do not think in a fleshly way of the colored rottenness of the flesh', which is our literal translation of this Bernard passage).

ingly would I be drained of life in order to enter perfectly into the stream of your divinity.

640 Ah, love, love, oh if only you perfected in me the festival of your nuptials; then my soul, snatched from the valley of misery, could be absorbed in its source just like a drop in the ocean. Ah, most dulcet Jesus, most cherished of my heart above everything that can be loved, and uniquely chosen one, be you my guide in this misery so that I may conclude my days in your praise and that I may finish my life 645 well, in your grace and friendship.

Ah, Jesus, dulcet love, be you the refuge for your poor spouse, who without you has nothing of her own nor anything good. In the great ocean of this age, be you her direction; and in the horrid tempest of death her consolation. Hold forth to me the hand of 650 your loving-kindness, and be you yourself the staff of my strength on which I may lean so firmly, O dulcet liberator of my soul, that all the deceits and insolence of my enemies may be reduced to nothing in the face of your might.

Ah, Jesus, my faithful friend, may the abyss of your generous 655 mercy be the safest hiding-place for me, in which I may escape the horrible insults of all my enemies. And you yourself be for me then my safe asylum, into which I may joyfully leap from the captivity of all evils. Ah, Jesus, my dulcet hope, may your deific heart (broken 660 by love for me) which lies uninterruptedly open to all sinners, be the first refuge of my soul out of its body. There, in the abyss of un-limited love, may my entire transgression be absorbed in a moment so that I may, without any obstacle, enter with you into the heavenly dance, O cherished one of my heart.

665 Ah, Jesus, my only salvation, my savior and my God, send to me in my last hour the faithful helper Mary, your lovable Mother, the renowned star of the sea,[118] so that, in the gaze of the red-glowing dawn of her glorious face, I may recognize you, the sun of justice,[119]

---

118. *Ave, maris stella* (Hail, star of the sea), a hymn to Mary dating back to the seventh/ eighth century, pictures Mary as the star of the sea showing the way to the seafarers on their voyage of life. Cf. Hermann Schulz, *Mittellateinisches Lesebuch* (Paderborn 1965) 76 (with the text of the entire hymn). The origin of *maris stella* may lie in the interpretation of the name 'Maria'. Cf. St Jerome, 'Liber de nominibus hebraicis', *Opera omnia*, PL 23 (Paris 1845) col. 842.
119. Ml 4:2 (3:20).

through the brightness of your light as you come near to my soul. Ah, cherished above all cherished ones, you know the desire of my 670 heart because you alone are the sighing of my soul. Ah, then, come more quickly so that I may utterly forget the pains of my heart in the presence of your lovable countenance.

Ah, love, love, observe the hour of my passing away and sign me with your seal; under your trustworthy guardianship, and out of 675 your exceeding goodness on which alone I lean, nothing can harm me in my soul. In my passing away, show your dulcet wisdom and strengthen my miserable soul so efficaciously that for eternity the soul may be refulgent with that exceeding compassion which you, renowned king, have through yourself wrought in it in my life and 680 death as well. Consume, then, all my vigor in your virtue and submerge me through your mercy in the abyss of deity where the lovable face of Jesus, the cherished of my heart, will satisfy me, warm me back to life, and fulfill me in your glory. Amen.

At this point, again commend your passing away and the end of 685 your life to God so that he himself may co-operate with you in all things[120] and in his mercy may order and arrange the end of your life, and say this prayer:

My God and my Lord, dulcet creator and my redeemer, in whom alone my heart has hoped, in whom I have believed, whom I have 690 confessed; O spring flower of divinity, sprinkle me with the dew of your ever-flowering humanity. May my soul be gladdened by the raindrops of your holy charity and gentleness, forgetting the evils of this exile. And, may [my soul], growing in you the sprouts of all virtues, O foremost gem and flower of virtues, calmly bear with you 695 my sojourn in this misery and act patiently in all tribulations and anxieties.

My God, my king, who are in the sanctuary where my life is hidden with my Jesus,[121] behold your chaste delights have overwhelmed me. Already I have perished from myself in you and, living, I have 700

---

120. Cf. Rm 8:28.
121. Col 3:3.

died. And now, where will I go from you? Both in heaven and on
earth, I now know nothing except you. My God, praise of Israel,
you who dwell in the sanctuary,[122] in whom I live and move and
have my being,[123] in you alone I trust. In you my heart is laid wide-
705   open[124] because you are my entire and only joy and all my desire.
The ray of your daylight has awakened my sleeping spirit.

Oh when will my soul be absorbed into the life-sustaining river of
your most dulcet and sempiternal fruition? Oh when will the deluge
of your love ravish my spirit and give me back to you to see your
710   mellifluous countenance, God of my life and author of my salvation
and keeper of my soul?[125] Without you I am nothing, nor know
anything, nor can do anything, nor am capable of anything; in you
alone I hope; to you I desire to come to see your most delightful
face flowing with life, to you I yearn to cling inseparably for etern-
715   ity, with all my heart, all my soul, all my virtue.

Ah! Consecrate my being and my life to your praise and glory
alone so that in all thoughts, words, deeds, and impulses of the rational soul, the marrow of my soul, and all the virtue and sub-
720   stance[126] of my body may praise and glorify you always in the
fullest charity and cherishing-love. The fact that my soul sojourns in
the prison of this body, desiring much, seething and gasping for
you, God, living fountain, and [the fact] that [my soul] is miserable
in this sojourn, ignorant of my entrance and exit; and the mere fact
725   that you, Father of mercies, neither disdain nor desert the work of
your hands[127]—may all this move to me the abyss of your compassion. Then, look upon my sojourn with the same viscera of mercy
with which you had pity on me when you deigned to experience
730   this same exile for thiry-three years and when, as if merciful to me,
you ransomed me on the cross—and your most dulcet heart was
broken for love.

---

122. Ps 21:4 (22:3).
123. Ac 17:28.
124. 2 Co 6:11; Ps 118 (119):32.
125. Ps 53:6 (54:4).
126. ExspSCh, 252, n. 1 here draws attention to the juxtaposition of *virtus* and *substantia*,
i.e. acting and being.
127. Ps 137 (138):8.

Ah! O most blessed life of my soul, be
my triumph and victory in all my temptations,
my patience in all weakness,
my consolation in all tribulation;
my total intention, beginning, end, and consummation in all
thought, word, and deed;   735
my holiness in all my life;
my perseverance in steadily waiting, to the very end of the good
fight.

Ah! O my very bright inheritance and best share of my soul, to
whom alone my expectation and my hope extend, at the hour of   740
my passing away, in your loving-kindness and clemency arrange and
order all that is mine so that the banner of your precious cross may
then be for me the firmest defense against all the crafty devices of
Satan; and let the very brightest arms of your victorious passion,
nails as well as lance, be for me the safest weapons against his thou-   745
sand frauds. Walled round by your triumphant and affectionate
death and signed[128] with the precious blood with which you have
ransomed me, with you as guide and provision for the way,[129] let
me cross over, unworried, through the narrow opening of death.

And then, do not forsake me, my salvation, but appear to me in   750
your charity, loving-kindness, and mercy in order that I may see
you face to face,[130] God, my lover, who created me for yourself.
There, O keeper of my soul,[131] dear Jesus, show me in the mirror of
manifest contemplation of you the glory of your divinity so that my
spirit and soul may be filled with your mercy and your splendid   755
praise and my heart may rejoice for eternity in you, O my dulcet
salvation.

And I personally, whom you have redeemed, will exult in the
goodness of your household, having been fattened with the marrow-rich cream of the fruition of your mellifluous face. I will be passionately glad and merry because I evaded the limitless crafty devices   760

128. Cf. Eph 1:13f.
129. Gertrud may allude here to the Viaticum.
130. 1 Co 13:12.
131. Ps 53:6 (54:4).

and snares of the devil, the flesh, and the world (and the anxieties of
death) and because I will possess you, O my most dulcet portion and
merriest life. There, you in me and I in you, clinging indivisibly to
765   you in eternal love, I assiduously praise your name for all the good
you have done to me, for you are the God of my life, the redeemer
and lover of my soul.

At this point, demand from the Lord the blessing and confirmation of his love, until you come to the vision of him:
770   O unifying love, God of my heart; love, praise, and jubilation of
my spirit. My King and my God![132] My cherished one, chosen out
of thousands.[133] Merriest spouse of my soul. Lord, king of virtues,
whom alone my heart cherishes, is fond of, and desires. Ah! O love,
God, you be for me yourself, meanwhile,[134] the dowry full of the
775   blessing of divine gentleness. Let my spirit cling to you in one spirit,
one breath, one will, one charity, until it becomes one spirit with
you for eternity. Fiery love, be for me yourself an efficacious and
living[135] blessing, dulcet and tuneful, in this my pilgrimage so that
780   my soul and all my virtue and substance, like a true spark,[136] may
burn, never to be extinguished, in the flame of your charity.

O living love, be for me yourself a consummating and perfecting
blessing, showing my soul to you as a worthy spouse. Let all my life
then be set in order in your charity; and let my death in you, O my
785   most blessed life, be fully consummated in the vivacity of faith,
hope, and charity and worthily prepared by all the sacraments of the
church. With all my vigor annihilated in your service and all my

---

132. Ps 5:3 (2).
133. Sg 5:10.
134. *Interim* (meanwhile)—significantly enough here used in the context of 'pilgrimage'—is a
term favored in medieval spiritual writing to denote life on earth while one awaits eternal life.
Cf. ExspSCh, 255, n. 6.
135. Similar formulations in St Bernard, SC 3.2, 29.8 and others.
136. Master Eckhart's notion of the *scintilla animae*, i.e. 'the divine spark' in the human soul
enabling us to a mystical experience, may in some germinal way form the basis for Gertrud's
metaphoric use of sparks of fire (see also IV, 341) or sparks of life (V, 452 and VII, 343).
While the term of the soul's divine spark is Eckhart's, the idea of a transcendental orientation
of the human soul has been a traditional one since antiquity (Cf. LThK 9 cols 1225f.).

viscera and marrow dried up in your love, let my soul, rid of the burden of my body—glad, unworried, and free—follow you, O my 790 dulcet loves, to the very intimacy, richness,[137] and radiance of the Holy Trinity. There, with all my sins remitted by your loving-kindness and my widespread transgressions fully covered over by your inestimable charity, my wasted life with its universal ruins will be replenished through you, O rich love, through the most perfect way of life of my Jesus. And there, my soul (here languishing and 795 wasting away because of the weariness of this life) will be rejuvenated in you, O life-sustaining love, and, renewed like an eagle,[138] and growing cheerful, it will exult; and, glad because of your mellifluous face, like one who has found and, now holding on, seizes the unlimited joys of eternal life which it will possess in you 800 forever, O God, love. Amen.

---

137. Literally: 'fatness'.
138. Ps 102 (103):5.

VII

LIFE IN DEATH[1]

WHEN IT PLEASES YOU TO CELEBRATE a day of making amends, collect yourself entirely within yourself at each of the seven hours[2] that you may be able to hold discourse with Love.[3] Delegate Love on your behalf to the Father of mercies[4] as if
5   to placate him, that, [drawing] on the treasure of his Son's passion, he may release you from your entire debt, even to the most recent point of your thoughtlessness. Then you may be unworried at life's end because you will have been fully released from all your sins.

And first, at lauds, you may read the first verse of this hymn:
10   Lift up the love of our mind
    To yourself, most kind,
    That our hearts be made clear
    By clemency drawn near.[5]

And add this: May your loving-kindness compel you to triumph
15   over our evil by pardoning [us]. And although I am unworthy to

---

1. 'Exercise of Making Amends for Sins and of Preparing for Death'.

2. This chapter is structured around the canonical hours, cf. Lauds (9ff.), Prime (69ff.), Terce (132ff.), Sext (192ff.), None (276ff.), Vespers (423ff.), and Compline (502ff.).

3. To address the divinity in prayer, Gertrud uses a number of allegorical figures in this chapter, i.e. personified Love, Mercy, Loving-kindness and others. It is noteworthy that most of these allegories picture the divine under the feminine aspect, such as *pietas* (Loving-kindness); *veritas* (Truth); *pax* (Peace); *sapientia* (Wisdom); *caritas* (Charity), *dilectio* (Cherishing-love). This important feature of medieval spirituality of understanding the feminine aspect of God cannot be adequately brought out in an English translation.

4. 2 Co 1:3.

5. We are indebted to Justin Lewis for his contribution to the translation of St Gertrud's verses in this chapter.

have my wishes granted, satisfy me, without hindrance, at the hour of death with your most dulcet countenance that in you I may find rest forever.

And so, in company with Mercy and Love, you will placate the Father with these words, saying with heart and mouth:

O dulcet Mercy of God, full of loving-kindness and clemency, 20 behold, miserable in the pain and anxiety of my heart, I take refuge in your lovingly-kind counsel because you are all my hope and trust. You have never disdained a miserable man. You have repulsed no sinner, however stinking. You have cast aside no man seeking refuge in you.[6] You have never passed by anyone in an anxious con- 25 dition without [showing] compassion. Like a mother you have always brought help to everyone in need. In accord with your name, you have stood in loving-kindness beside all those invoking you. Ah, and do not throw me, an unworthy woman, away from you because of my sins; do not repulse me because of my useless way of life. 30

Do not disdain me, nor say of me: Why should she still occupy the ground?[7] Rather, in accord with what you are by nature, care for me in a lovingly-kind, lovingly-kind way. Behold, set up in extreme impoverishment of merits, I come, I come to those hospices full of charity for the poor who are in you, lest I die in the open air 35 under the cold and rain of my unfruitful life. [I come] hoping that from your generous hand I may be given alms through which my wasted life may be repaired. And there, with the fleecy wool of your great compassion, warm my naked body that your charity may cover over all my sins and make amends for all my negligence. 40 Ah, open to me your secure dwelling-places that I may be saved by your grace. Through you, may the lovingly-kind charity of God help me, in which alone the health of my soul and spirit is secure.

Ah, O Love, Love, look upon my Jesus, this royal hostage of yours, marked with the diadem of mercy, whom you have seized at 45 this hour with such violence that you, one with him, might claim as your own all his goods, enriching heaven and earth with this your

6. Cf. Jn 6:37.
7. Lk 13:7.

noblest booty and refilling everything with good out of the abundance of your most glorious hostage.

50   Ah, with this dearest spoil, with this hostage whom you cherish a thousand times over, redeem my wasted life for me and make restitution to me for my useless way of life, not just sevenfold but a hundredfold. For, even if I alone had the life of all human beings and angels, it would still not be possible for me to be valued at a price

55   such as that which your very desirable hostage is worth; how much less when I am a vile human being, dust and ashes.

    Oh, if my wish were granted that, with Jesus, the best beloved, you captured and bound me and treated me, a little woman, as your own heir! By consorting and discoursing with this divine hostage,

60   from a sinner I would be made into a saint; from one useless into a truly spiritual human being; from an enemy into a true friend of God; from one lukewarm into someone truly thirsting for God; from one barren and unfruitful into one sprouting the perfection of all virtues and the holiness of all religion. There, my dear Jesus, may the bosom of your mercy be the prison of my captivity. There, let

65   the chain of your divine heart be my bond in such a way that, in the violence of living love, I may become your prisoner[8] forever, indivisibly glued to you, living entirely for you and clinging to you so that, for eternity, I may never be capable of being separated from you. Amen.

70   At the hour of Prime, hold discourse with Love and Truth so that while they are speaking on your behalf at the hour of death you may come to judgment unworried, having the judge himself, Jesus, as your lovingly-kind advocate and respondent.

Verse:
Kind Lord, you know
Us sinful and slow,
75   Made from mere earth,
Wretched from birth.

---

8. This is another passage where the female perspective is obvious in the Latin original. The sinner, the saint, the enemy, the friend, the prisoner, and the adjectives lukewarm and unfruitful are all given in the feminine gender.

May your loving-kindness compel you to triumph over our evil by
pardoning [us]. And although I am unworthy to have my wishes
granted, at the hour of death satisfy me, without hindrance, with
your most dulcet countenance that in you I may find rest forever.

And so begin to placate God:

O dear Truth, O just fairness of God, how will I appear before
your face bearing my iniquity, the guilt of my wasted life, the   80
weight of my exceedingly great thoughtlessness? I have not, alas,
alas, paid the coin of christian faith and of spiritual life to the money
dealers at the table of charity, where you might receive it as you
wish, together with its increasing earnings of total perfection. Not
only have I spent in idleness the talent of time entrusted to me, but I   85
have also lost it, treated it perversely and squandered it altogether.
Where will I go, where will I turn myself, and where will I flee from
your face?[9]

O Truth, you have justice and fairness as indivisible associates.
You judge all things by number, weight, and measure.[10] Whatever
you seize, you lift onto an exceedingly just scale. Woe to me, a   90
thousand times woe, if I were handed over to you without an advocate to answer for me. O Charity, may you be my deputy.
Answer for me. Obtain indulgence for me. Act in my cause so that I
may live by your grace.

I know what I will do; I will take the chalice of salvation.[11] I will   95
place Jesus' chalice on the empty scales of Truth. Thus, thus, I will
make amends for everything I lack. Thus, I will fully cover over all
my sins. With this chalice I will fill all my ruins. With this chalice I
will make amends even more than adequate for all my imperfection.

Ah! O Love, this your royal vanquished one, my Jesus, has been   100
weakened to the very marrow of his being by the agitation in the
viscera of your mercy. It was at this hour that you dragged him with
such violence to judgment that you might impute to him (who had
no spot, save the cause of his love for me) the sin of the entire world
and my [own] guilt, expiation for which you exacted from him. Ah,

---

9. Ps 138 (139):7.
10. Ws 11:21.
11. Ps 115 (116):13.

105   let me receive from you today, O dearest Love, as my partner in
        judgment this most innocent, this dearest one, condemned for the
        love of my love and sentenced to death on my behalf. Give me such
        a hostage that I may have him as defender of my entire cause.

110   O dear Truth, I would find it unbearable to come to you without
        my Jesus; but how exceedingly delightful and lovely to appear
        before you with my Jesus. O Truth, be seated at the tribunal now;
        enter now the council chamber and reveal about me whatever you

115   please. I will fear no evils;[12] I know, I know that your face will by
        no means confound me while he, my great and total trust, is with
        me. I would like to know what sentence you could pronounce
        against me now when I have my Jesus with me, the dearest, the
        most faithful one, who has borne my misery for the sake of obtaining
        great mercy for me.

120   My most dulcet Jesus, lovable pledge of my redemption, come
        with me to the judgment. Ah, let us stand together. Be my judge
        and advocate. Explain in detail what you have done for me, how
        well you have thought of me, at what a high cost you have ransomed
        me that through you I might be justified. You have lived for me lest

125   I perish. You have carried my sins. You have died for me lest I die
        eternally. You have conferred your all on me that I might become
        rich in merit through you. Ah, at the hour of my death, judge me
        by that innocence, by that spotlessness that you conferred on me
        when, though yourself judged and condemned on my behalf, you

130   delivered me from all my debt so that, however poor and needy I
        am[13] in myself, I might have all good in abundance through you.

        At the hour of Terce, consult with Peace and Love that the pith
        and marrow of your senses may for eternity be consecrated to the
        Lord and that at the hour of death you may thereby be found fully

135   reconciled to God. And say:
        Let my cause to you be known,
        To whom no thought remains unknown.
        Sweep away our lying dreams,
        All this world that only seems.

---

12. Ps 22 (23):4.
13. Ps 85 (86):1 Cf. St Bernard, SC 1.4.

May your loving-kindness compel you to triumph over our evil by　140
pardoning [us]. And although I am unworthy to have my wishes
granted, at the hour of death satisfy me, without hindrance, with
your most dulcet countenance that in you I may find rest forever.

O Peace of God, which surpasses all our understanding,[14] pleasant
and lovable, dulcet and so unwavering; wherever you come, there is
imperturbable security. You alone can bridle the sovereign's rage.[15]
You make comely the king's throne with clemency. You brighten
the kingdom of the imperial glory with your loving-kindness and　145
mercy. Ah, defend my cause, accused and poor as I am. Ah, receive
me under your wings so that there I may be protected[16] from
menacing evil, which I fear because of my much and great thoughtlessness.

Behold, the creditor already stands at the door reclaiming from
me the deposit of my life. The tax collector exacts from me the pay-　150
ment of my time; although it is not safe for me to speak with him
when I have nothing with which to deliver myself from debt. O my
Peace,[17] most dulcet Jesus, how long will you be silent? How long
will you be secretive? How long will you say nothing? Ah, rather
speak for me now, saying a word in charity: I will redeem him.[18]
Surely, you are the refuge of all those who are miserable. You pass　155
by no one without a greeting. You have never left unreconciled
anyone who has taken refuge in you. Ah, do not pass me by without charity, miserable and hopeless as I am. Placate the Father for
me. Receive me into the bosom of your charity. Hold out to me a
drink of the cool water of holy hope so that I may be able to live. O　160
Charity, make my tongue cool. Recreate my soul, now almost fainting from impoverishment of spirit.

Ah, Love, Love, at this hour my Jesus was for me crowned with

---

14. Ph 4:7.
15. The image evokes Plato's bridling the horses in *Phaedrus* 254.
16. Ps 16 (17):8.
17. Eph 2:14.
18. This paragraph abruptly shifts from the feminine perspective employed throughout the
text to a masculine one. In two passages, Gertrud applies words of a masculine gender
presumably to herself: the pronoun *eum* (him) in line 155 and the modifiers *miserum*
(miserable) and *desperatum* (hopeless) in line 158. Perhaps St Gertrud inadvertently relapses into
the male *persona* commonly used also by nuns in prayer and the liturgy.

thorns, and intoxicated with loving-kindness. You made Jesus, my
165   true king, without whom I know no other, an outcast among
humankind, rejected and disdained[19] like a leper, so that Judea
would deny he was hers; but, thanks to you, I have him for my very
own. Oh, if only you would give me my Jesus, the most innocent,
the dearest (who for me so fully repaid what he had not robbed[20]) as
170   an arm for my soul that I might receive him into my heart, warming
my spirit to life again with the bitterness of his pains and suffering.
Ah, that that bitterest discipline of my peace[21] which you imposed
on him might pay for all my negligence and debt.
175   O Peace, be my dear bond to Jesus forever. Be my dearest pillar of
strength; bound to you in indivisible friendship, let me become one
heart and soul with Jesus. In you, O most dulcet Peace, I will take
to myself the scourges of charity, the intimate wounds of love;
through you I will remain glued to my Jesus forever. O Peace, let
180   me have yet one little word: Open to me that worthiest alabaster
box of love that is stored with you and which, with its scent of life,
may awaken my listless spirit.
Oil and anoint my senses with the blood streaming from that
most glorious head, with the pain of [his] venerable senses that by
185   that balsamy savor I may be altogether transformed from idleness
and torpor of my spirit, just as earth's barrenness is exchanged in
springtime for its new flowers. Ah, my most dulcet Jesus, may the
actions of your holiest senses totally conceal my guilt and make
190   amends for all my thoughtlessness. Then whatever I lack I may have
entirely in you, who have expended yourself entirely for me. Amen.

At the hour of Sext, you may hold discourse with Wisdom and
Love so that all that you are may be renewed and [that] at the hour
of death you may be defended by virtue of Christ's precious cross
195   from all temptation and the crafty devices of the enemy. And read
this verse:

---

19. Cf. Is 53:3.
20. Ps 68:5 (69:4).
21. Is 53:5.

As strangers to this world we come,
In exile groaning for our home.
Harbor and homeland us provide,
And to life's entrance do us guide.
May your loving-kindness compel you to triumph over our evil by   200
pardoning [us]. And although I am unworthy to have my wishes
granted, at the hour of death satisfy me, without hindrance, with
your most dulcet countenance that in you I may find rest forever.
O wondrous Wisdom of God, how powerful, how very bright is
your voice. Without exception you call to yourself all who yearn
for you. You indwell in the humble. You cherish those who cherish
you.[22] You judge the cause of the poor. You show lovingly-kind
mercy to all. You hate nothing of what you have made.[23] You keep   205
secret the sins of human beings, and you mercifully await their repentance.[24] Ah, open for me, too, the vein of life, giving me a drink
from the cup of indulgence that I may know what is acceptable with
you at all times.[25]

O Wisdom, you wield the holy sign of never-ending life in your   210
right hand; for you everything follows prosperously. You and you
alone are able to do all things. Abiding in yourself, you renew all
things. Ah, renew me in yourself and make me holy that you may
be able to transport yourself into my soul. You set up the friends of
God[26]; ah, ransom God's friendship for me. Cause me to watch for   215
you in the morning that I may truly find you.[27] Take possession of
me that I may truly yearn for you.

Oh, how prudently you go about setting things in order. Oh, how
providently you arrange all things when, by way of saving human-

---

22. Pr 8:17.
23. Ws 11:25.
24. Ws 11:24.
25. Ws 9:10.
26. Gertrud does not use this phrase (see also VII, 61) in the restricted sense of The Friends of God, which is the name of a fourteenth century religious movement in the Rhineland. Cf. LThK 4 cols 1104f. and DSp 1 col. 493. Rather, Gertrud understands any person who trusts in God's loving friendship as a 'friend of God'. Cf. also Doyère (*Legatus* I and II (139) 50): 'le terme . . . ne désigne encore qu'une orientation du zèle spirituel . . . '. and in *Legatus* III (143), 368: 'Les Amis de Dieu'.
27. Is 26:9.

220   kind, you come around the king of glory, going to him with your
        most prudent counsel. Directing him to think of peace and to fulfill
        charity while maintaining his princely majesty, you have laid on his
        back an opportunity for love that he might bear on the wood the in-
        iquity of the people.[28] Ah! and ah! O very bright Wisdom of God,
225   whose magnificent works no diabolical malice could impede; whose
        lovingly-kind counsels all the ignorance of human depravity could
        not change; whose multitudinous mercies, whose magnitude of
        love, and whose fullness of goodness no magnitude of offences could
230   quench. Rather, your imperial assiduousness would prevail, pleas-
        antly arranging all things, reaching strongly from end to end.[29]
            O Wisdom, most outstanding virtue of divine majesty, if only
        your efficacy prevailed over me, an unworthy woman. If only, with
        the breath of your mouth, you were to blow upon and annihilate in
235   me, small as I am, all hindrances to your will and gracious purpose,
        that through you I might conquer all temptations, and through you
        overcome all hindrances, that in the greatness of love, dying to
        myself, I might live in you. Under your guidance I will evade well
        the shipwreck of this life, accept from you the shelter of charity and
240   the cover of cherishing-love, and establish with you a covenant of
        living love.
            O Wisdom, what a game you bring to perfection, what a joke
        you play on my Jesus. You lay bare the king of glory, making him a
        spectacle of abuse. You affix to the trunk of a tree the price of the
        entire world. You alone weigh and mark out how much value this
245   mystery has in paying the debt for all transgressions. From the earth
        you lift up on the cross the life of all that he, drawing everything to
        himself[30] in his death, might make them live.
            O wise Love, what a remedy you prepare so that universal ruin be
        filled. Oh, what a plaster you apply to cure the wound of all. O
250   Love, your counsel is help for those who are lost. You condemn the
        blameless man to save the miserable culprit. You pour out innocent
        blood to be able to placate enraged justice and to ransom the

---

28. 1 Pt 2:24.
29. Ws 8:1.
30. Jn 12:32.

Father's clemency for the poor and needy.[31] O wise Love, your
motto is relief for those who are miserable. You plead the cause of   255
peace. You heed the importuning mercy. By your prudent counsel
you bring help for the anxiety of all through the most gracious will
of your clemency. You impose an end to universal misery through
the glorious work of your mercy. O Love, what you have devised is
the opportunity for salvation for those who are lost.   260

Behold, O Wisdom, your pantry full of loving-kindness is already
open. Ah, look upon me, the culprit, standing outside the door of
your charity. Ah, fill the little cloak of my poverty with the blessing
of your gentleness. Behold, before you is the empty little cup of my
desire.[32] Ah, may the latch of your fullness open. Teach my heart   265
your chaste counsels, your lucid precepts, your faithful testimony.[33]
Make me remember your commandments to observe them.[34] Ah,
do not treat me according to my sins nor repay me according to my
iniquities,[35] my Jesus. Ah, just as you have truly been favorable to   270
me with your blood, so also by virtue of your precious cross, make
restitution to me for all the wastefulness of my life. Ah, O wise
Love, shelter and cover over my negligence. Make amends for me
for all my negligence through my Jesus, abandoned by free will to
your judgment.   275

At the hour of None, you may hold discourse with Love and
Cherishing-love (so that they may entirely exchange their good for
your evil and envelop your death in the death of the Lamb) that
under such tutelage, you may cross over unworried. And say the
verse:

Made a pauper for our sake,   280
A criminal—nailed to a stake.
With your side's blood you wash away
The evil of our yesterday.

---

31. Ps 85 (86):1.
32. Ps 37:10 (38:9).
33. Ps 18 (19):8.
34. Ps 102 (103):18.
35. Ps 102 (103):10.

May your loving-kindness compel you to triumph over our evil by pardoning [us]. And although I am unworthy to have my wishes granted, at the hour of death satisfy me, without hindrance, with your most dulcet countenance that in you I may find rest forever.

285 O beautiful Cherishing-love of God. O zealous striving for Charity stronger than death.[36] You are the healing of creation, the salvation and redemption of all the world. Oh, how dulcet your conversation. Oh, how pleasant your colloquy. In living with you there is no tedium. Consort with you is true joy[37] without end. Ah, enter into

290 my mean little bedchamber and rest with me. Make me hear your colloquies, full of the Holy Spirit, that, with you, I may forget all my anxiety and tribulations. Be with me on this way where I walk because all good things come to me in your company.[38]

O honorable Cherishing-love, behold me, a miserable little being,

295 driven about by the most powerful wind of my thoughtlessness and terrified by the thunderous awareness of my sins: Beneath the shelter of your loving-kindness I take refuge because I sense that no hope is left for me except in you, and I find rest nowhere outside of you. Like a mother, you foster the lost man at your bosom. In your

300 exceedingly farsighted and ripely considered counsel you play with the Son of the most high to the very [moment] of death; and, in order to bring help to a miserably desperate man, you do not spare him.

O Charity, O Cherishing-love, for sinners you have done such a thing with the Virgin's Son that you have given all desperate people

305 hope in you. Through your own graciousness you compel everyone to act trustfully toward you; and, so that none who are miserable may have a cause to plead against you, you turn the cause of all to salvation. O Charity, prepare for me, a destitute and derelict woman, a place of counsel in you, a nest of refuge, where my afflicted spirit

310 may recline. Endure with me the cause of my sojourning here. Raise my fainthearted spirit. Relieve the anxiety of my heart by saying to me: I will not forget you.[39] Ah, in saying so, let your word be invio-

---

36. Sg 8:6.
37. Cf. Ws 8:16.
38. Ws 7:11.
39. Is 49:15.

late, O Charity, and deign to call me to your calends because my
soul yearns passionately for market days when, at your lovingly-
kind markets, you may exchange with me my evil for your good.   315
You hold my gentle salvation (my dear Jesus) so strongly fastened to
the cross that, giving up his spirit under your hand, he dies for love.

O Charity, what are you doing? Whom are you assaulting? You
neither spare [anything] nor rest until at length you bring help to   320
those who are miserable. You do not measure love. You so afflict
the fountain of life⁴⁰ with thirst that to die once does not suffice [for
him]; but dying now he so exposes himself still further to love⁴¹ that
he yearns and thirsts for dying a multiple death—[death] for each
one—redeeming those lost with a more costly pledge. O Love, your
assiduousness has touched the nerve of my Jesus' heart so energeti-   325
cally that it withered away broken for love.⁴² O Love, may it suffice
you now, may you set a measure now that my Jesus hangs dead
before your eyes. Dead, plainly dead, that I might have life more
abundantly.⁴³ Dead that the Father might adopt me more dearly as
a child; dead that I might live more happily.   330

O dearest death, you are my happiest lot. Ah, let my soul find a
nest for itself in you, O death. O death, bearing the fruits of eternal
life, ah, may your life-giving streams envelop me totally. O death,
everlasting life: ah, may I always have hope under your wings.⁴⁴ O   335
saving death, ah, may my soul linger in your very bright goodness.
O most precious death, you are my dearest ransom. Ah, may you
absorb all my life in you and immerse my death in you.

O most efficacious death, ah, let my death be safe and carefree⁴⁵   340
under your care. O life-giving death, ah, may I melt beneath your
wings. O death, drop of life, ah, may the very dulcet spark of life

40. Ps 35:10 (36:9).

41. This paragraph contains a Latin wordplay with *mors, mori,* and *amor* (death, dying, love)
that the English translation cannot imitate.

42. Gn 32:25.

43. Jn 10:10.

44. Ps 90 (91):4.

45. To come close to the Latin wordplay *secura-cura,* we have here translated 'carefree' when
we normally use 'unworried'.

you bring burn in me forever. O glorious death. O fruitful death. O
death, the sum of my whole salvation, the lovable contract [leading]
345   to my ransom, the firmest pact [leading] to my reconciliation. O
triumphant death, dulcet and life-giving, in you shines forth for me
such charity whose equal has not been found in heaven and on earth.

O death, very close to my heart, you are my heart's spiritual trust.
350   O most loving death, in you are all good things stored up for me.
Ah, may your lovingly-kind care be with me so that in dying I may
repose dulcetly beneath your shadow. O most merciful death, you
are my happiest life. You are my best share. You are my most copious redemption. You are my very brightest inheritance. Ah, en-
355   velop me altogether in you, hide my life altogether in you, hide my
death away in you.

O death diffusing gentleness, provide for my death: in my anxiety
over death, enclose me totally. Through you, let me cross over not
worrying that robbers will beset my passing away. At your bosom,
360   with those you ransomed most dearly, collect my spirit again. Receive
my soul on the couch of your fullest charity, absorb my life into
you, immerse me totally in you. O dear death, prepare a rest then
for me in you. Make me breathe out my spirit happily and pleas-
365   antly fall asleep in you. O death very close to my heart, preserve me
then for you forever in your fatherly charity as a ransom and sempiternal possession.

O Love, you have ransomed that health-giving death for me, my
dearest lot. You have done such great and good things for me that
370   you have tied me to you in servitude forever. What shall I repay
you[46] for such unlimited good? What praise and thanksgiving could
I offer to you even if I expended myself a thousand times? What am
I, a vile little being, to you, O my copious redemption? Let me then
375   offer you my entire soul that you have redeemed; let me confer
upon you the love of my heart. Ah, may you transfer my life to
you. May you carry me totally away in you and, enclosing me in
you, make me one with you.

O Love, the ardor of your divinity has locked for me the very

---

46. Ps 115 (116):12.

dulcet heart of my Jesus. O heart that diffuses gentleness. O heart 380
that runs over with loving-kindness. O heart that overflows with
charity. O heart that distills pleasantness. O heart full of compassion. Ah, make me die of love and cherishing-love for you. O
dearest heart, I pray from my heart, absorb my heart totally in you.
Dearest pearl of my heart, invite me to your life-sustaining banquet. 385
Give me, an unworthy woman, the wines of your consolation to
drink. Fill the ruins of my spirit with your divine charity, and let the
abundance of your charity make amends for the destitution and impoverishment of my mind.

O Love, if only you now offered that heart for me, that most
dulcet aromatic thyme, that most pleasant incense, that worthiest 390
sacrifice on the golden altar[47] of human reconciliation, as amends
for all my days that I have lived without having brought you any
fruit. O love, immerse my spirit in the flow of this mellifluous heart,
burying in the depth of your divine mercy the total weight of my in- 395
iquity and thoughtlessness. Give back to me in Jesus the brightest
understanding and the purest affection so that through you I may
possess a heart set apart from all carnality, detached and free that at
the hour of death, under your guidance, I may reassign a spotless
spirit to God. 400

O very beloved heart, my heart now cries out to you. Remember
me: let the gentleness of your charity refresh my heart, I beseech
you. Ah, let the marrow of your compassion be moved on my
behalf because, alas, I have many bad demerits [and] no good
merits[48] at all. My Jesus, let the merit of your precious death, which 405
alone was effective in paying the universal debt, give me pardon in
you for my demerits whatever they are, and give back to me in you
all the good things I have lost. Turn me back to you so efficaciously
that, transformed deep inside myself through the violence of your
divine love, I may find that grace in your eyes and may obtain that 410

---

47. Cf. Rv 8:3.
48. A passage very similar to this one (including the repetition of *bona merita* and *mala
merita*) may be found in St Augustine's *Liber de gratia et libero arbitrio* VI. 14 (*Opera omnia*, vol.
35, 1835, 476). (ExspSCh, 286, n. 3.).

mercy which you merited[49] for me when, dying for the sake of the love of my love, you expired on the cross. And grant me, dear Jesus, to love you alone in all things and above all things, to cling to you fervently, to have hope and to have exceeding hope in you.

415   As for the rest, grant me to act worthily in response to your death. At the hour of [my] death, let me merit experiencing without any delay the most dulcet fruit of my redemption and the very worthiest merits of your death with as great an efficacy as you yearned for for my sake when, in thirsting for my salvation, you breathed

420   out your Spirit and redeemed me at the great price of your blood. O Love, at my death may you bid me a dulcet farewell so that I may rest pleasantly in peace in you. Amen.

At Vespers, come together with Love and Loving-kindness to placate God so that, at the termination of life, they may answer for

425   you to the Lord for all your debt and imperfection. And read this verse:

Who thirsts but happy Charity
For you, life's fountain:[49a] verity.
How blessed are the eyes of all
Whose glances dare upon you fall.

430   May your loving-kindness compel you to triumph over our evil by pardoning [us]. And although I am unworthy to have my wishes granted, at the hour of death satisfy me, without hindrance, with your most dulcet countenance that in you I may find rest forever.

O dulcet Loving-kindness of God. O dear liberality of God. You open your bosom to all; you are the refuge of the poor. O Loving-kindness, what do you counsel? Where will I flee from the face of the cold, being already incapable of bearing the roughness of winter?[50]

435   The lukewarmness of my rational soul has already constricted all the ploughed lands of my heart with icy cold. Ah, shade me with your

---

49. Because of the emphasis in this paragraph on 'merit', we have translated *mereri* as 'merit' (otherwise as 'deserve').
49a. Jn 35:10.
50. Cf. Mt 24:20.

shoulders, covering up the nakedness that confounds me. May I then warm myself and take hope beneath [your] wings[51] for eternity. O Loving-kindness, Loving-kindness, do not desert me, an anxious woman. Do not avert your face from my sobs and cries. May   440 your charity compel you to hear me patiently. Ah, open your bosom, where I may repose a little and pour out my spirit in your presence. [I am] certain that, because of your goodness and the loving-kindness that is part of your nature, you do not spurn a desolate woman or disdain an afflicted one. Oh how suitable your conduct is to those in misery. Oh how agreeable already are the   445 scents of your perfumes to those almost fainting away.

You raise the stricken; you deliver the shackled.[52] You disdain no man in tribulation; you look upon the need of all maternally and mercifully. You counsel those in despair with loving-kindness. To everyone's indigence you bring help most clemently. Ah, now bend   450 your ear to me, an indigent woman, that I may hold rare discourses with you for the sake of my soul and may receive dear counsel from you.

Behold, I become passionately alarmed by what I have committed; I blush very much at what I have omitted; I become exceedingly frightened at the wastefulness of my life. I fear that future investiga-   455 tion at which Christ, a noble man,[53] will impose a reckoning on me. If he wanted to exact a deposit from me for my time and interest from the talent of understanding he conferred on me, I would, in short, not find any worthy answer for your charity.

What will I do? Where will I turn? I lack the strength to dig; I   460 should blush to beg.[54] O Loving-kindness, Loving-kindness, speak up now; may your dulcet counsel, I entreat you, warm my spirit back to life. Ah, answer me: what does it seem to you I should do in this [situation], for according to your name you have a truly lovingly-kind heart and you know best what may be expedient for me in all this. Ah, pardon me and bring me help; and in this tribulation,   465

---

51. Ps 90 (91):4.
52. Ps 145 (146):7–8.
53. Lk 19:12.
54. Lk 16:3.

do not be detached from me. Let the poverty of my spirit move you and, touched by the compassion of your heart, say to me with loving-kindness: May there be one purse for me and you.[55]

470 O Loving-kindness, Loving-kindness, you have stored up with yourself riches so immeasurable that heaven and earth do not suffice to contain them. You have driven my Jesus to give his soul for my soul, his life for mine, so that you might make everything that was his mine; and thus, out of your abundance, this pauper's substance might increase. Ah, call my starved soul to your food supply so that

475 in this life I may live from your riches and, reared by you and nourished by you, may not grow faint under the discipline of the Lord until at length, under your guidance, I turn back to my God and give my spirit back to him who gave it.[56]

O loving-kindness, O goodness, O dulcet liberality of God, you

480 have stored in your repository a certain wondrous dower which stuns heaven and amazes earth, the like of which will not be found again throughout the ages. Daily on the altar you offer for me such a sacrifice to God the Father, such a holocaustal incense, that it goes beyond all merit and is truly capable of paying all my debt. You pre-

485 sent again to the Father a Son truly pleasing to him that you may placate him toward me and truly reconcile [me to him].

Ah, through this mystery, which best can make amends for my imperfection and make reparation for all my defects, make my life new and restore to me a hundredfold all that I have wasted so that

490 my soul may exult in you;
my youth like an eagle's may be renewed in you;[57]
my life may be turned back to you;
my entire virtue may serve you;
my whole substance may glorify you.

My Jesus, by your loving-kindness destroy all my iniquities;[58] by your charity cover over and hide all my sins; by your cherishing-love make amends for my negligence; by your love reestablish me in

---

55. Pr 1:14.
56. Si 12:7.
57. Ps 102 (103):5.
58. Ps 50:3 (51:1).

that freedom of spirit by which you, the heir[59] of innocence, have   495
set me free, dying for me by giving the price of your own blood.
Make me conform to your will so that I may transform my life in
you. Make me completely whatever you want me to be so that after
this life, having left behind the cloud of my body, I may in jubila-   500
tion see your mellifluous face.

At Compline, hold discourse with Love and Perseverance so that,
having exchanged your vile way of life for the worthiest life of the
Lord Jesus, you may be found through him, at the hour of death,
fully consummated in all holiness and perfection of religion. And   505
read this verse:
How great the glory of your days
And all the memory of your praise.
This they endlessly proclaim,
Whose hearts rise up with one sole aim.   510
May your loving-kindness compel you to triumph over our evil by
pardoning [us]. And although I am unworthy to have my wishes
granted, at the hour of death satisfy me, without hindrance, with
your most dulcet countenance that in you I may find rest forever.
O persevering Charity of the Lord Jesus, who has cherished us up
to the very [moment of] death, you alone wear the diadem of the
kingdom. To you is due the triumph of victory, the title of glory.
Your farseeing diligence, your diligent guardianship, confers upon   515
the King of kings[60] such gifts that heaven is stunned.
O persevering Charity, truly your voice is dulcet and sonorous,
your face pleasant and comely. You gather from the wasteland
dowers so rare, and virtues so many in species and aromas that with
a cheerful countenance the God of heaven reveres your face [while]   520
yearning for and praising your beauty[61] and radiance. Before all else
God aids you[62] with his countenance, for in your midst he is not
disquieted [and] he rests like a spouse in the inner chamber. Ah, aid

---

59. Mt 21:38.
60. Rv 19:16; 1 Tm 6:15.
61. Cf. Ps 44:12 (45:11).
62. Ps 45:6 (46:5).

me at the morning's daybreak,[63] O true noonday,[64] preserving my
525   soul in you from the blindness [that comes] at every twilight.

O persevering Charity, you are the perfection of all virtues and
the sanity of spirit. You make heavy burdens light: you make the
labor of all virtues dulcet by your good use; and your habitual use
makes it merry. O perfect charity of God, in you is all gentleness
530   and pleasantness. You are true peace and security. In you is imperturbable peace and tranquillity. You are the end and consummation
of all goodness, the fulfillment of God's commandments. You are
the sabbath of sabbaths. In you, wisdom deepens its inactivity; in
you love perfects its activity.[65]

535   O persevering Charity, in my Jesus you consummated the work
that loving-kindness enjoined on him.[66] You fuliflled the work of
our redemption, recalling the lost back to the lot of adoption. You
make my Jesus fall pleasantly asleep in peace, rest in you from labor,
540   repose beneath your shadow, have a dulcet sabbath holiday, and,
locked and buried under your seal, capture the sleep of love.

O Charity, under your guardianship, under your ever-watchful
diligence, you preserve the chosen price of my soul, well beloved
above gold and topaz,[67] who alone can redress all my defects and
545   remedy all my imperfection. Ah, there where you preserve stored in
you my dearest treasure, there place and store my heart, too, so that
through you my entire spirit may abide there where my dearest
dear one dwells.

550   O unconquered Charity, O strong Perseverance of the Lord Jesus,
from the depth of my heart the cry of my spirit rises to you. Ah, act
as my ambassador; speak well for me. [It is] in you [that] my Jesus,
my king and my God, perfected the work which the Father gave into

---

63. Ibid.
64. See also St Bernard, SC 33.6: *O vere meridies.*
65. St Bernard, SC 68.2, also contrasts *otium* with *negotium*. Gertrud's paragraph is replete
with words that traditionally evoke the idea of contemplation: *securitas* (security), *tranquillitas*
(tranquillity), *pax* (peace), *sabbatum* (the sabbath), *otium* (idleness). In the following paragraph
the verbs *obdormire* (fall asleep), *quiescere* (rest), *pausare* (repose), and *sabbatizare* (observe the sabbath) have the same effect.
66. Jn 17:4.
67. Ps 118 (119):127.

his hands to do. Also through you may I, vile little worm, be given a   555
pure heart and an unconquered spirit with which to serve him diligently and with faithful zeal and, under the yoke of love, to persevere in carrying his commandments on my willing shoulders. Then
you, O efficacious Love, may be my true requital a hundredfold[68] in
life as well as in death, and I may receive you as my prize, for in you
is my total and full joy.   560

Make me, in loving contrition and humble repentance always,
like a little dog, gnaw on my sins and on the imperfect works caused
by my defects so that, after this life, I may receive that most dulcet
crumb,[69] the most dulcet fruition of the mellifluous face of my
Jesus. And then, through you, let me be satisfied in eternal gladness   565
when the glory of my Jesus appears.[70]

O stable Love, strong and insurmountable, may your sagacity
teach me to cherish Jesus with unconquerable steadfastness and to
serve him with unconquered perseverance. And, aroused by you
and agitated by you, may I always be prepared when my Lord   570
comes in the first or second watch[71] so that I may not be listless or
sleepy when the cry is made at midnight,[72] but, moving forward
with you and under your guidance, may I worthily enter into the
nuptials with the Lamb. Ah, and then with you taking care of me,
let my lamp be found full of the oil[73] of charity, full of cherishing
conflagration, full of the splendid light of the works of living faith   575
that, through you, I may possess the delights of eternal life.

My most dulcet Jesus, much beloved spouse, revive my listless
spirit in you now; in your death restore to me a life lived for you
alone. Grant me a way of life corresponding worthily to the price of
your blood. Grant me a spirit that savors you, senses that sense you,   580
a soul that understands your will, virtue that perfects your gracious
purpose, and stability that perseveres with you. Ah and at the hour

---

68. Mt 19:29.
69. Mt 15:27.
70. Ps 16 (17):15.
71. Lk 12:38.
72. Mt 25:6.
73. Mt 25:4.

of death, open to me without delay the door of your most gracious
585 heart that through you I may merit entering without hindrance into
the inner chamber of your living love, where I may enjoy and have
you, O true joy of my heart. Amen.

On the same day, when you celebrate making amends (as previ-
ously mentioned), at noonday pray the Lord to lead you into the
pleasure garden[74] of his divine heart that you may bathe there seven
590 times in the Jordan of the merits of his life and passion and that, on
the day you depart this life, purged from every spot, all beautiful,[75]
you may be led into the inner chamber of his divine love.

Ah, Jesus, my living salvation, who, beautiful and very bright,
595 [come] from the land of angels, alas, alas, my soul, your cherished
creation, abides darkly in blindness. Ah, be my salvation and direct
enlightenment. My cherished one, by the pure tears of your
brightest eyes, wash away all spots of the sins of my eyes, that, at
the termination of my life, without hindrance and with the clean
600 eye of my heart I may see your most dulcet face in the mirror[76] of the
Holy Trinity, for you alone are the one I desire with all my heart.
Ah, submerge me more quickly into the abyss of my fruition of you.

Ah, Jesus, my lovable hope, spouse faithful and full of mercy, you
605 never spurn the sighs of those who are miserable—alas alas, through
my own vice my ear has grown deaf. Ah, O Father of mercies,[77] let
my life obey you once my ear hears you. My cherished one, by the
dulcet loving-kindness of your blessed ears wash away all iniquity
from my sinful ears so that, at the hour of death, I may not fear
610 hearing evil news[78] but may hear your most dulcet calling with joy
and gladness,[79] for you alone are my expectation. Ah, take me away
more quickly to marriage with you.

---

74. Cf. Dn 13:7.

75. Sg 4:7.

76. St Gertrud's use of the mirror image is basically influenced by 1 Co 13:12. This particular passage belongs to the complex mirror imagery (mostly based on Ws 7:26) in the
writings of the mystics. Cf. Margot Schmidt, 'Lumière au moyen-âge', DSp 10/2 cols
1290–1303 [passim].

77. 2 Co 1:3.

78. Ps 111 (112):7.

79. Ps 50:10 (51:8).

Ah, O eternal gentleness of the soul, uniquely cherished of my
heart, whose face is full of all lovableness and [whose] heart of all   615
pleasantness—alas, alas, my thought wanders away from you. Ah,
O God of my heart, may my disordered mind be collected again on
you. My cherished one, through the pure intention of your holiest
thinking and the burning love of your heart pierced-through, wash
away all the guilt of my evil thoughts and of my slanderous heart so   620
that your most bitter suffering may shade me in death, and your
heart, broken for love, may be my everlasting dwelling-place, for
you alone are the cherished one to me above all creation. Ah, do
not suffer my being removed from you for a long time, uniquely
cherished one of my heart.   625

Ah, Jesus, only-begotten of the heavenly Father, lovingly-kind
and merciful Lord, you never leave your adopted children behind in
desolation—alas, alas, much have I transgressed with my tongue.
Ah, O my glory,[80] fill my mouth with your praises.[81] My cherished
one, through the lively might of the dulcet words of your blessed   630
mouth, wipe away every offense from my defiled mouth so that,
glad in the kiss of your mellifluous peace, I may cross over from this
age, for your mellifluous mouth alone can console my innermost
heart.[82] Ah, radiant love, pierce my heart with the dart of your living
cherishing-love that I may fall drained of life into the abyss of the   635
source of your life.

Ah, Jesus, wisest workman, most outstanding maker, you have so
laudably restored the work of your hands which I have destroyed—
alas, all my works are imperfect and not in accordance with your
law. Ah, O my refuge and virtue,[83] let me work with[84] your living   640
love to make all my work holy in you. My cherished one, through
the perfection of your works and the crucifixion of your hands,
wash away every offense from my unloving, unkind hands so that,

80. Ps 3:4 (3).
81. Ps 70 (71):8.
82. Cf. Sg 1:1.
83. Ps 45:2 (46:1).
84. Elsewhere in this text *cooperatio* appears as 'co-operation'. To follow contextual links
among several terms related to 'work' in lines 637–642, we have translated it as 'work with' at
this place. In all cases, *cooperatio* means 'working with' God and God 'working with' us.

645   without hindrance at the hour of death, I may rush into your very dulcet embrace with no delay, for you are my legitimate spouse, chosen out of thousands.[85] Ah, at the final hour, acknowledge me as your own, not because of my merit but because of your innate goodness.

    Ah, Jesus, lovable youth, loving and desirable, whose companion-
650   ship is so noble and so much to be wished for—alas alas, I have turned aside from the right way, and I have not kept your commandments. Ah, O my dear guide, direct my steps according to your will. My cherished one, through the painful weariness and the divine perfora-tion of your blessed feet, wash away every spot on my sinful feet so
655   that through you, O faithful escort on my road, I may march gladly into the place of the wonderful tabernacle, even to the house of God,[86] because you are the unique prize that I run for.[87] Ah, bestow on me a love that does not allow me to act in a lukewarm or
660   negligent way but impels me to run after you untiringly.

    Ah, Jesus, great God, dulcet and gracious, who do not know how to give except great things. Ah, living God, whose fiery inflow draws back to his bosom everything that ever flowed out from you— alas, alas, all my life rotted away, withered up, and decayed. Ah, O
665   God of my life, may my life in you become green again, begin to flourish again, and grow strong [in producing] worthy fruits. My cherished one, through the noble innocence of your life and your pure holiness, wash away all the filth of my corrupt life that my life may already be no longer with me but, in the fiery vigor of your love, may be totally carried away with you. And then, at the hour
670   of death, I may happily find myself in you, O my true life, for you are my supreme and much cherished good and the one and only refuge of my soul. Ah, grant I may languish for you out of love, die out of desire, praise you with jubilation, and be eternally consumed in the conflagration of your charity. Amen.

---

85. Sg 5:10.
86. Ps 41:5 (42–43:4).
87. 1 Co 9:24.

In the evening, as if picking flowers with the cherished one, pray   675
for blessing[88] and for these virtues:

May your soul bless me today, I entreat you, dear Jesus. May
your imperial divinity bless me. May your fruitful humanity bless
me so efficaciously and your royal munificence leave behind for me
such visible signs of your blessing that, totally changed from myself   680
into you by unconquerable love, I may cling to you inseparably.
Make me perfect in fearing you. Make me pleasing to you

in humility of spirit,
in brotherly charity,
in chaste simplicity,
in humble shyness,
in cleanliness of heart,   685
in the guarding of my senses,
in sanctity of life,
in ready obedience,
in dulcet patience,
in spiritual discipline,
in willful poverty,
in holy leniency,
in maturity of conduct,
in cheerfulness of spirit, and
in all truth,
in good conscience,
in steadfastness of faith,
in holy perseverance,
in strength of hope,   690
in fullness of charity, and
in the blessed consummation of your cherishing-love:

so that the thornbush of my heart may be converted into a paradise
of all virtues and a red berry bush of total perfection, as if it were a

---

88. In this passage, Gertrud follows the pattern of similar liturgical benedictions, notably the
blessing given by the bishop at the end of the Consecration of the Virgins ceremony. Cf. *Pontificale*, 146.

field full of all peace, holiness, and loving-kindness that the Lord has blessed.[89]

695   Ah, Jesus very closest to my heart, always be with me in such a way that my heart may abide with you and your love may indivisibly persevere with me, and thus may my passing be blessed by you and may my spirit, set free from the shackle of the flesh, from then on rest in you. Amen.

---

89. Gn 27:27

INDEX OF SCRIPTURAL CITATIONS

[Line numbering is keyed to the *Exercitia spiritualia* (Sources Chrétiennes text) and approximated in the English translation.]

Genesis (Gn)

2:23	VI 435
7:11	IV 336
18:27	VI 15
19:19	VI 322
27:27	VII 694
32:25	VII 325f.
32:26 (28)	IV 48f.; V 500

Exodus (Ex)

15:11	III 14f., 88f.
23:20	I 76
33:11	IV 117

1 Kings (1 K)

8:11	VI 8

1 Chronicles (1 Ch)

17:20	VI 329

Tobit (Tb)

12:15	VI 539f.

Esther (Est)

1:7	III 98

2 Maccabees (2 M)

1:4 (4–)	I 94f.

Job (Jb)

7:17	III 93f.
9:3	VI 38
10:9	VI 151
19:25–26	VI 154f.
19:27	V 470
23:3	III 58f.
35:5	VI 56f.
38:7	VI 539f.

Psalms (Ps)

1:4	IV 315
3 (4):3	VII 629
4:7 (6)	I 18; II 57
4:9 (8)	V 224, 462f.; VI 83f.
5:2 (1)	VI 172
5:3 (2)	VI 771
5:5 (3)	V 19
8:4 (3)	VI 363
15 (16):8	I 122
15 (16):11	V 275, 445
16 (17):8	III 164; VII 146f.
16 (17):15	VII 565f.
17:2–3 (18:1–2)	V 95f.
17:3–4 (18:2–3)	IV 255ff.
17:30 (18:29)	V 283f.
17:36 (18:35)	I 65
17:41 (18:40)	IV 383
18 (19):8	VII 266f.
18:11 (19:10)	V 163, 482; VI 227
20:4 (21:3)	VI 493f.
20:7 (21:6)	III 155
21:4 (22:3)	VI 702f.
22 (23):1	VI 496
22 (23):4	VII 114
22 (23):5	VI 532f.
23 (24)	IV 75
23 (24):6	IV 76f.
25 (26):7	V 475
26 (27):3	V 413f.
26 (27):6	VI 165f., 318
30:6 (31:5)	V 522
30:17 (31:16)	VI 549
30:21 (31:20)	V 442
33:6 (34:5)	IV 66f.
33:9 (34:8)	I 104; V 485f.
34 (35):3	V 139
34 (35):10	VI 352

147

WORD INDEX

[Line numbering is keyed to the Latin edition of the *Exercitia* (Sources Chrétiennes) and approximated in this English translation.]

abundance (*abundantia*) III 246, IV 352, VI 280, VII 49, 387, 473

abyss (*abyssus*) III 97, 193, IV 87, 336, 338, V 300, VI 238, 331, 378, 484, 655, 662, 682, 726, VII 602, 636

adopt(ion) (*adoptio/adoptare*) I 221, III 218, V 305, 510, VI 531, VII 329, 537, 627

affect(ion) (*affectus/afficere*) I 235, II 36, 109, IV 53, 205, 326, V 2, 6, VI 192, 193, VII 397

age (*saeculum*) II 90, III 205, 303, IV 194, V 44, 99, 280, VI 601, 648, VII 481 (2x), 632

aid (*adiutorium*) I 62, IV 90, 91 (*adiuvare*) I 31, 82, 130, III 346, IV 285, V 164, 403, 417, 518, VII 522, 523

almighty/almightiness (*omnipotens/omnipotentia*) I 30, 110, 216, II 60, 102, III 115, 308, 311, IV 5, 23, 317, V 118, 514, VI 389, 530

altar (*altare/ara*) V 94, VI 75, 129, 521, VII 391, 483

amends, making amends, amending (*suppletio/supplere/supplementum*) I 192, III 186, IV 58, 173, 352, V 4, 507, VI 2, 163, 453,VII 40, 97, 99, 190, 273, 387, 392, 487, 495, 588

angel (*angelus*) I 70, 71, 74, 77, 78, III 7, 127, 207, 294, 316, IV 107, VI 95, 123, 267, 317, 365, 457, VII 54, 594 (*angelicus*) III 128, 229—archangel (*archangelus*) III 127, IV 107

annihilate (*adnibilare*) IV 326, V (39), VI 788, VII 234

anointing (*unctio*) I 151, II 54, IV 31, V 294, VI 131

anxiety (*angustia (e)*) VI 133, 404, 573, 697, 761, VII 21, 25, 257, 292, 311, 358

armor, arms, armed (*armatura/arma/armatus*) I 108, 199, IV 382, VI 744

ashes (*cinis*) V 154, VI 15, 355, VII 56

aspect (*aspectus*) IV 289, V 273, VI 291

beauty/beautiful (*pulchritudo/pulcher*) I 210, III 69, 294, 378, IV 35, 153, 252, 412, V 45, 68, 74, 102, 141, 150, 242, 341, 460, VI 297, 340, 585, VII 285, 521, 592, 594

bedchamber (*cubiculum*) III 229, V 103, 139, 397, VII 290—inner chamber (*thalamus*) III 128, 174, 229, 274, IV 159, V 134, 397, VI 82, 89, VII 523, 586, 592

blessing (*benedictio*) I 49, II 12, III 223, 232, 318, 329, 375, IV 22, 82, V 231, 325, 360, 500, VI 493, 494, 775, 778, VII 263, 676, 680

blindness (*caecitas*) I 44, IV 175, VII 525, 595

blood (*sanguis*) I 19, 146, 178, 180, II 59, III 13, 39, 77, 219, 278, 292, V 508, VI 410, 468, 747, VII 252, 270, 420, 497, 580

body (*corpus*) I 78, 150, 178, 180, 181, 193, 204, 206, II 10, 75, 98, III 38, 43, 56, 84, 103, 125, 178, 191, 199, 200, 242, 251, 291 (2x), IV 96, 107, 142, 183, 190, 305, V 248, 281, 283, 456, 531, VI 88, 100, 290, 393, 596, 612, 615, 619, 632, 661, 719, 721, 790, VII 500

152

CISTERCIAN PUBLICATIONS INC.
Kalamazoo, Michigan

TITLES LISTING
THE CISTERCIAN FATHERS SERIES

Texts and Studies in the Monastic Tradition

Temporarily out of print   † *Forthcoming*

THE CISTERCIAN STUDIES SERIES

MONASTIC TEXTS

CHRISTIAN SPIRITUALITY

MONASTIC STUDIES

CISTERCIAN STUDIES

Saint Gregory Nazianzen: Selected Poems

Eight Chapters on Perfection and Angel's Song
(Walter Hilton)

Creative Suffering (Iulia de Beausobre)

Bringing Forth Christ. Five Feasts of the Child
Jesus (St Bonaventure)

Gentleness in St John of the Cross

Distributed in North America only for Fairacres Press.

DISTRIBUTED BOOKS

St Benedict: Man with An Idea (Melbourne Studies)

The Spirit of Simplicity

Benedict's Disciples (David Hugh Farmer)

The Emperor's Monk: A Contemporary Life of
Benedict of Aniane

A Guide to Cistercian Scholarship (2nd ed.)

*North American customers may order
through booksellers or directly from
the publisher:*

Cistercian Publications
St Joseph's Abbey
Spencer, Massachusetts   01562
(508) 885-7011

*Cistercian Publications are available
in Britain, Europe and the Common-
wealth through A. R. Mowbray &
Co Ltd   St Thomas House   Oxford
OX1 1SJ.*
*For a sterling price list, please consult
Mowbray's General Catalogue.*

*A complete catalogue of texts-in-
translation and studies on early,
medieval, and modern Christian
monasticism is available at no
cost from Cistercian Publications.*

*Cistercian monks and nuns have been
living lives of prayer & praise, meditation
& manual labor since the twelfth century.
They are part of an unbroken tradition
which extends back to the fourth century
and which continues today in the Catholic
church, the Orthodox churches, the
Anglican communion, and most recently,
in the Protestant churches.*

*Share their way of life and their search for
God by reading Cistercian Publications.*

Cistercian Publications
Editorial Offices
WMU Station
Kalamazoo, Michigan   49008
(616) 387-5090